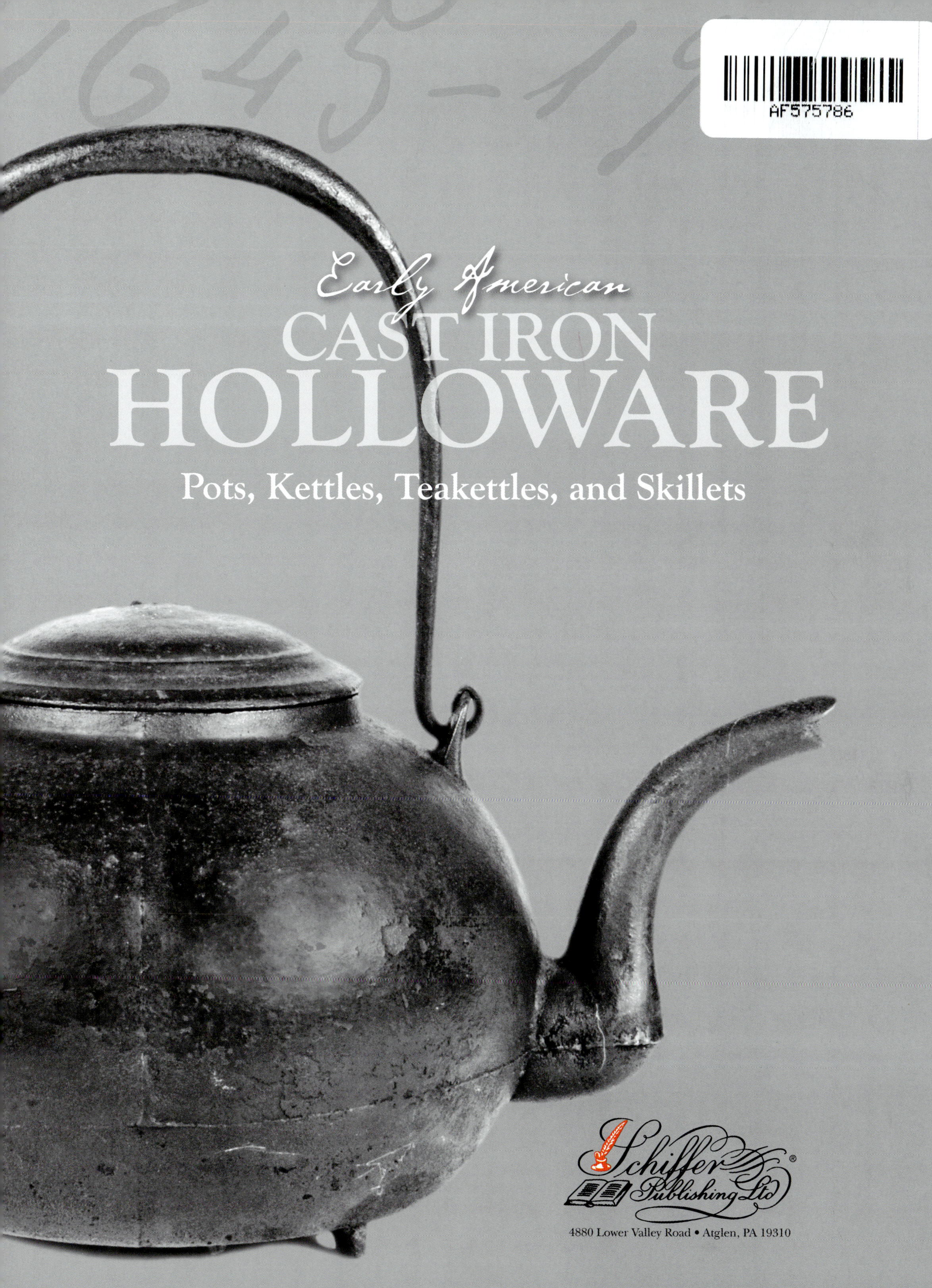
1645–1
Early American
CAST IRON
HOLLOWARE
Pots, Kettles, Teakettles, and Skillets
Schiffer Publishing Ltd
4880 Lower Valley Road • Atglen, PA 19310

Library of Congress Control Number: 2013950034

Designed by Danielle D. Farmer
Type set in Goudy Oldstyle/P22 Cezzanne/Aviner

ISBN: 978-0-7643-4536-4
Printed in China
5 4 3 2

Published by Schiffer Publishing, Ltd.
4880 Lower Valley Road
Atglen, PA 19310
Phone: (610) 593-1777; Fax: (610) 593-2002
E-mail: Info@schifferbooks.com

To Roger Tyler, who was employed as the founder at the Hammersmith Ironworks, established by John Winthrop Jr. at Saugus, Massachusetts, in 1646, and his coworkers who operated the first successful blast furnace on the American continent.

ACKNOWLEDGMENTS

Thanks first to Keith Francis, whose perceptive eye spotted many of the examples herein and from whom they were obtained. John Mehl has also alerted me to many pots on the Internet, some of which are now in this collection. Longtime friend Dave Kohler has a similar interest in old iron and from time to time has sent me materials he has discovered, many from sources unfamiliar to me. One of Dave's leads included early French pots illustrated in *Tunica Treasure* by Jeffrey Brain. The complete book was later loaned to me by Jon Mehl.

A special thank you to Theresa Hurley, Chief Librarian at the Lynn, Massachusetts, Public Library for permission to photograph the Saugus Pot, held as a valued relic by the library.

To Carl Salmons-Perez, Cultural Resources Program Manager and to Janet Regan, Museum Technician at the Saugus Ironworks National Historic Site, Saugus, Massachusetts, many thanks for enabling me to examine pot fragments excavated from the first ironworks. This extensive collection has provided important clues to the form of early pots. Appreciation also goes to Ann Wagner, Curator of Metals, and Susan Newton, Photographic Services Coordinator at the Henry Frances duPont Winterthur Museum, Winterthur, Delaware, who provided information and photographs of the Saugus pot in that collection. Thanks to Leslie LeFevre-Stratton, Curator of Collections at the Huguenot Historical Society, New Paltz, New York, who graciously allowed a large pot, possibly from Saugus, to be photographed for the study. Tom Kelleher, Curator at Old Sturbridge, Massachusetts, provided information related to the Ellis Griffith pot, which is a duplicate of two similar pots in their collection. Further information on the iron industry of Carver, Massachusetts, was provided by the Carver Public Library.

Artist Kim Stone added clarity with her pen and ink drawings to illustrate the blast furnace and various pot features. Irwin Richman has been a friend for many years. His various publications on Pennsylvania Dutch culture have provided inspiration to produce this book. Thanks are also due to the many antique dealers from whom I have bought pots over the last forty years. I am particularly grateful to Mary Ann Bollinger and Dennis Cox, who found time amid busy schedules to read the manuscript. Their comments and corrections have enhanced the book. Errors that remain are my own.

Finally, a very special thanks to my wife Darlene, who has tolerated an ever-increasing amount of ironware and the drain on the wallet to acquire it. Without her computer and photographic skills, this book would not have taken shape.

—John Tyler

CONTENTS

INTRODUCTION

This book is the result of forty-five years of collecting and researching cast iron holloware pots, kettles, Dutch ovens, teakettles, skillets, and frying pans. Hollowware, because each requires the use of an inner core mold to produce a hollow vessel, is a more involved and technically demanding process than is needed to cast a flat plate such as a stove plate.

Between 1971 and 1978 the author wrote three periodical articles that could be considered preliminary studies for this book. They appeared in *The Magazine Antiques*, August 1971; *Winterthur Conference Report 1973: Technological Innovation and the Decorative Arts; and Early American Life*, April 1978. Since then, a collection of more than two hundred examples has been gathered with the aim of acquiring those which illustrate changes over time in form and casting details denoting changes in casting technology. Some bear initials or other marks enabling specific identification of maker, place, and time; most do not. One must therefore carefully note details of changes in form and casting marks that offer clues to changes in the technology of manufacture that can be related to specific dates. In most cases these changes are minor but significant. In some ways the process is akin to the archeological technique of comparing pot shards of known dates and origins at one site to those found at another site to infer sources and dates.

To many collectors and antique dealers, a "gypsy pot" is a type of vessel covering a wide range of dates. They do not look closely to discern details that may be clues to age. Seventeenth century vessels have been found in antique co-ops surrounded by twentieth century "collectibles." Frequently, late nineteenth century pots and kettles are found in museum restorations of colonial fireplaces and kitchens. Hopefully this study will enable curators and collectors to more accurately determine the age and provenance of American and some foreign holloware.

All vessels illustrated are of cast iron unless otherwise noted. Those in chapter one are copper alloy. The vessel in chapter two is wrought iron. Unless otherwise noted, all examples are from the author's collection. Terms that may be unfamiliar to the reader will be found in the glossary.

Chapter 1

Before Cast Iron: VESSELS OF COPPER-ALLOY METALS

Copper-alloy metals, bronze, and brass, were known and produced in antiquity. Bronze, an alloy of copper and tin, sometimes with lead, originated about 2000–2500 BC in the Middle East. Brass, an alloy of copper, zinc, and sometimes calamine, appears to have originated in Mesopotamia around 1000 BC. Brass was more fully developed in the Roman era.[1] Smelting from raw ore developed about 4000 BC in Western Asia.[2] Prior to this time copper was used in its native, unsmelted form.

Hammered-copper vessels of ancient forms are still made in Turkey. Bronze and brass cast vessels were made and used well into the nineteenth century in Britain, Europe, and America. Early bronze age vessels were made of beaten copper or bronze sheets riveted together in a spherical form.[3] These usually employed opposed ring-handles for lifting. Frequently they are depicted sitting over a fire on a three-legged stand or trivet. Small vessels might be hammered from a single sheet.[4] Some were also made of hammered wrought iron sheets joined with rivets like the bronze or copper vessels and of similar form.[5]

Cast copper-alloy vessels were in use in Europe by the thirteenth century.[6] By the fourteenth and fifteenth centuries brass-casting and bronze-founding industries had become large enough to divide into specialized groups, including "potters" who cast pots, cauldrons, and household articles.[7]

The earliest cast-bronze or brass vessels were lost-wax castings in which each pot was molded individually in wax over a clay core. The wax formed the space of the wall thickness of the vessel, plus the legs and ears or handles. An outer clay layer completed the mold. A central rod passing through all three elements maintained the correct alignment of the core with the outer mold. Vessels were cast bottom-up and the rod was vertical. When all was prepared, the mold was heated and the wax ran out, leaving the cavity between the inner and outer mold to be filled with molten metal, poured in through a leg or foot opening.[8]

Vessels cast in this way may have a plugged hole in the bottom center where the rod previously was fixed. Spherical vessels such as pots may be irregular in form if the clay core and wax body were shaped by eye rather than on a rotating potter's wheel against a template. (See page 10, top.)

An early method of applying the wax was to lay it over and around the core in strips, the marks of which may be seen on the interior walls of some pots.[9] Early pots were modeled after pottery forms and tended to be spherical with rounded ears.[10] The lost-wax method of casting was time consuming and tedious. It was most suitable for statues and irregularly shaped works of art.

Most pots and cored vessels of the fifteenth through the seventeenth centuries were cast using

- The early use of copper-alloy vessels preceded cast iron vessels.
- The earliest cast copper-alloy vessels were lost-wax castings.
- The loam molding of vessels in molds of baked clay was a tedious and time-consuming process leaving tell-tale marks on the finished product.

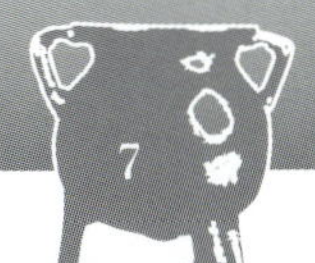

the loam-molding method. The loam-molding technology was essentially the same for brass, bronze, or iron cast vessels. Details related here apply to cast iron vessels as well. This method was used until early in the eighteenth century. In this process, cord or rope was wound around a tapered spindle until a mass sufficient to form most of the pot interior was reached. It was then coated with loam or clay and rotated against a wooden template to form the core mold for the hollow interior. This was baked over a fire and dusted with finely pulverized charcoal, which enabled the next layer to separate cleanly from it. The second layer was applied and also shaped by rotating the loam against a template. This layer took the space of the actual vessel wall. After another dusting, a third layer was applied which constituted the outer mold.

While still pliable, the third layer was slit from the rim down to the bottom and back up to the rim on the opposite side, cutting the outer mold into two halves. Clay ear and foot molds formed using wooden patterns were applied to the outer mold and it was then baked. The inner middle layer was scraped away, leaving the space for the molten metal.[11]

The spindle was drawn out of the core and the hole it left was plugged and smoothed over. The spindle hole through the outer mold served as a sprue or opening through which molten metal was poured into the mold. It was extended several inches by a clay funnel. Large vessels often used two sprues placed at opposite sides from the center, enabling two men to pour metal into the mold simultaneously, filling it more evenly and quickly.

The two halves of the outer mold were set around the core mold "bottom-up" on a board. Chaplets, small pieces of like metal of proper thickness to maintain the correct distance between core and outer molds, were carefully placed. These are often visible on the finished casting as round, square, or hexagonal plugs. The assembled mold was bound together and buried in the earth to hold the halves together against the pressure of the molten metal.

Sand casting was used during the seventeenth century for bronze and brass kettles and skillets.

The vessel was then cast. When sufficiently cooled, but not cold, it was lifted up and the outer mold was broken away. The core was pulled out and the core mold removed. The long, tapered extension of the sprue was chiseled off, leaving a round stub (or stubs if multiple sprues) on the bottom of the pot.

The loam-molding technique was used until Abraham Darby perfected sand casting for iron pots in 1707.

The distinctive mark of loam-molded bronze or iron pots is the vertical seam on the outer surface dividing the vessel in half, the trace of the two halves of the outer mold.[12] (See page 12.)

Often in making copper-alloy vessels, legs, handles, and ears (the L-shaped lugs for the bail) were cast separately and brazed on. Sometimes they were cast as one with the vessel. Ears were set at rim level or slightly lower. They were usually located at right angles to the vertical mold line, but were not always equidistant in this fashion. One leg was positioned under an ear and the other two equidistant from it.

Ears might be rounded on very early vessels or angular. By the seventeenth century, the ear might have its top length horizontal with a curve to the pot shoulder. Angular ears of the seventeenth and early eighteenth century may slope down from the rim.

Prior to the nineteenth century, legs were frequently faceted with four, five, or six sides ending in hoofed feet. Some had grotesque mascarons on the upper leg surface.

The explorer LaSalle had an apparently similar pot according to Father Hennepin's 1683 account where mention is made of a small metal pot with the face of a lion. Indians he encountered considered this to be formidable "medicine."[13] (See page 12.)

Some vessels lacked legs in order to be easier to transport slung at the saddle bow of a nomad owner. They could be set over rocks at a campfire.[14] (See page 9.)

Sand casting, that is, the casting of bronze and later iron products in sand-filled, multi-part molding boxes, called flasks, using a pattern to produce the vessel shape was not known prior to 1400. It became common in the seventeenth century. The earliest description of the process is in the treatise *Pyrotechnia* by Biringuccio, 1540. [15]

With this method, using a brass, wood, iron, or pewter pattern vessel, an identical product could be made each time. Instead of breaking a laboriously made clay mold to remove the vessel, one simply re-packed especially cohesive sand around the pattern within the multi-sectioned molding box, which could be used over and over. Skillets and kettle forms, having no undercuts, were simple to mold in this fashion and are among the earliest vessels cast by this method. Some seventeenth-century skillets and a very few late seventeenth-century pots were cast in sand molds. At this time no iron vessels were sand cast, only those in bronze or brass.[16]

Pot, bronze or brass, Mediterranean or Middle East, undetermined age. Height 6.25", rim diameter 5.625". Cast and crudely lathe turned.

Pot, copper, wrought iron, Turkey, ca. 1850–1920. Height 6.5", rim diameter 8.25", hammered copper with tinned interior, wrought iron bail ending in snake heads has a center cusp in sixteenth to seventeenth century style. Some Norse bronze cauldrons take the same form.[17] Viking voyagers to the Middle East may have transferred this form to Europe.

Interior showing marks of wax strips used in lost-wax process.

Ears cast separately and brazed on after the body was turned.

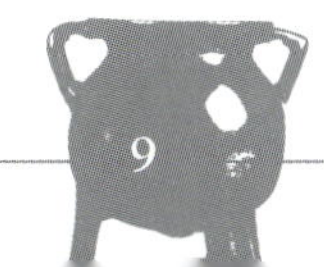

Legs individually molded with toed feet are each different.

Pot, brass, Europe, ca. 1300–1400. Height 5.875", rim diameter 3.5". Round form lost-wax casting derived from pottery types.[18] Body hand molded (not turned), rounded ears for finger grips, plug in bottom.

Pot, bronze, the Netherlands, ca. 1300–1400.[19] Height 3.25", rim diameter 2.5". A miniature lost-wax casting with angular ears cast separately and brazed on after the body was cast. Shortened legs.

LEFT to RIGHT:

Pot, bronze, Low Countries, ca. 1400–1500.[20] Height 5.75", rim diameter 3.875". Loam molded with legs and ears brazed on. Slipper foot. Heavy wear on ears from bail.

Bottom showing remains of sprue.

Pot, bronze, Germany or the Netherlands, ca. 1400–1600.[21] Height 9.875", rim diameter 13.75". Marked "AO" under rim. All cast marks have been removed from this vessel. This wide, shallow form was probably used on a German style raised hearth.

Pot, bronze, wrought iron, German, ca. 1550. Height 8.5", rim diameter 6". Loam molded with visible vertical parting lines and sprue. Angular ears. Legs cast separately and applied are hexagonal in section with bearded mascarons and hooved feet. Original heavy wrought iron bail.

LEFT to RIGHT:

Pot, bronze, wrought iron, German, ca. 1500–1700.[22] Height 8", rim diameter 9.75". Loam molded with triangular-section legs removed. Angular ears. Twisted wrought iron bail. Typical pouch-shaped German form. Modern trivet.

The mark "IK" has not been identified.

Pot, bronze, English, ca. 1650. Height 9.25", rim diameter 11". Bears the casting mark of William Sturton I of Somerset, England.[23] Loam molded and of typical seventeenth century angular slope-sided English form also found in cast iron pots. Eroded legs have flat backs and molded fronts. Lip repaired.

The ears of this period are angular and typically slope down from the rim on English pots, but not on Continental examples where the top bar usually extends straight out from the rim.

Mark scratched in the clay mold of the Sturton Foundry.

Skillet, bronze, English, seventeenth century. Height 5", rim diameter 8". Marked "IH3" on reeded handle swelled at end. Legs worn to stubs, sprue on bottom. Possibly made by John or Joseph Hatch or John Higden.[24] Texture of molding sand remains on exterior.

Skillet, bronze, possibly Scandinavian, ca. 1650–1700. Height 3.625", rim diameter 4.75". Sand cast, sprue filed off. Curved round-section legs end in slipper feet. The tubular handle is depicted as early as ca. 1410 in European art.[25] Coarse filed surface finish.

Legs and handle are brazed on. Toed foot pads, which extend around the front and back of the legs, are also typical of French cast iron vessels.

Skillet, bronze, probably French, ca. 1650–1750. Height 5.375", rim diameter 7". The wide, flat-bottom form is typical of earlier skillets,[26] but the molded rim suggests an eighteenth-century date.

The crude boxlike receptacle for a wooden handle seems to be a later repair. Sand cast with sprue on bottom.

Skillet, bronze, American, possibly Boston, Massachusetts, ca. 1800. Height 4.25", rim diameter 4.125". Sand cast with filed outer surface. Sprue on bottom.

Undercuts at joins of legs and handle show they were brazed on. Marks where three legs were incorrectly placed and then removed remain on the bottom. One leg is always under the handle. The rejected leg placement had none in that position.

Skillet, bronze, English, ca. 1780–1816. Height 4", rim diameter 4.75". Handle marked "WARNER 1P". Tomson Warner of London carried on the family business from 1780–1816.[27] Sand cast, sprue on bottom, handle and D-section legs brazed on. Legs marked "1P" on back indicating leg pattern for one pint skillet.

Skillet, bronze, American, ca. 1790–1820. Height 5.75", rim diameter 11.75". The Frederick, Maryland, area where this skillet was found had copper mines and refining and manufacturing facilities by 1780.[28] Sand cast. Outer surface left rough. Other sizes with similar features are found in the Pennsylvania–Maryland border region.

The long handle was brazed to a cast-in stub. Triangular-section rim. Legs are four sided with chamfered corners, cast with the body. Sprue filed off the bottom.

Kettle, bronze, wrought iron, American, Frederick, Maryland, area, ca. 1790–1820. Height 5.75", rim diameter 11.75". Sand cast and lathe turned to smooth surfaces. Rim of triangular section same as previous example. Flat wrought iron handle with bean pads riveted on.

Chapter 2

WROUGHT IRON VESSELS

The earliest iron vessels were made of wrought iron plates or sheets bent to shape and riveted together. Small vessels could be hammered into rounded forms from one sheet; larger sizes were composed of several sheets. They were generally semi-circular in form with two flopping ring handles on opposite sides near the rim.[1]

Wrought iron was produced by the smelting or reduction of iron ore in a bloomery forge fire using charcoal as a fuel. The ore was broken up into small pieces and layered with charcoal in the forge hearth. As the iron oxide in the ore was reduced by carbon-monoxide from the fire, semi-molten iron settled to the bottom of the hearth pit along with slag formed from impurities in the ore. This mass of pasty iron and slag was then removed and hammered into a bar or plate.[2] During the hammering process, the molten, glassy, slag was physically expelled from the iron. The result was wrought iron, low in carbon content and having a fibrous, wood-like structure due to the slag incursions, which were elongated by hammering. It was a tough metal that resisted bending and when beaten thin was still very strong.

Iron was being produced by this method in Europe by 600 BC.[3] As time went on, other methods and refinements altered this process in detail, but not in its basic elements. Prior to the introduction of the blast furnace to produce cast iron in Europe in fourteenth century France and in England in the late fifteenth century,[4] iron vessels were made of wrought iron, hammered and riveted together, not cast in molten metal.

The earliest iron vessels were made of hammered wrought iron sheets produced at a bloomery forge. These were then shaped and riveted together.

CLOCKWISE:

Pot, wrought iron, Turkey (?), ca. 1900. Height 5.0625", rim diameter 6.375". Sheet iron wrapped and riveted with vertical seam, inset rim. Vessels made in this manner have been found in Viking burials.[5] A swivel allows the pot to rotate over the fire.

Though a late example, this pot illustrates the earliest technique of forming an iron vessel.

The bail is formed of a flat strip bent over and shaped into pads at the ends, which are riveted to the pot. It has traces of a punched chevron design on the top surface.

Chapter 3

CAST IRON POTS

Cast iron vessels were produced by the smelting of iron ore in a blast furnace to generate molten metal, which was then ladled into molds. When the iron solidified, the finished products of pots, kettles, tea kettles, and skillets could be removed. To produce cast iron in the blast furnace, iron ore, charcoal, and limestone were layered inside a shaft that tapered in at the top and bottom where a smaller hearth area was located. Carbon monoxide from the burning charcoal, brought to a smelting temperature by a forced air blast, reduced the iron oxide in the ore to a liquid iron-carbon-silicon alloy, which fell into the hearth area as molten iron. The limestone reacted with impurities in the ore to form slag, which also fell to the hearth and floated on top of the molten iron. Prior to tapping the furnace, the slag was drawn off. The iron was tapped every twelve hours[1].

Cast iron, produced in a blast furnace and poured into molds, allowed the mass production of holloware. Pot casting in England had begun by 1543. Pot casting increased throughout the seventeenth century, although the products remained quite heavy.

BLAST FURNACE KEY

1. Tunnel Head opening for charging the furnace.
2. Heavy Outer Stone-Masonry Stack.
3. Alternate layers of limestone, ore, and charcoal charged through the tunnel head.
4. Sandstone or brick inwall.
5. Rubble, sand, and clay fill between inwall and stack allows for expansion with heat.
6. Casting or Working Archway.
7. Bosh. Widest part of the furnace supporting charge of materials above. Here iron ore and slag begin to become molten and descend into the crucible.
8. Tuyere Arch.
9. Tuyere Nozzle admitting air under pressure to crucible promoting combustion.
10. Timp Stone spanning opening of fore-hearth.
11. Crucible where smelting temperature reaches 1500° C.
12. Damstone retaining molten iron and slag in hearth.
13. Fore Hearth. Molten iron was taken via hand ladles from this area to the molds where casting took place.
14. Molten slag floats on top of the molten iron and is periodically drawn off through a notch in the dam stone.
15. Molten iron.
16. Sandstone Hearth Stone.

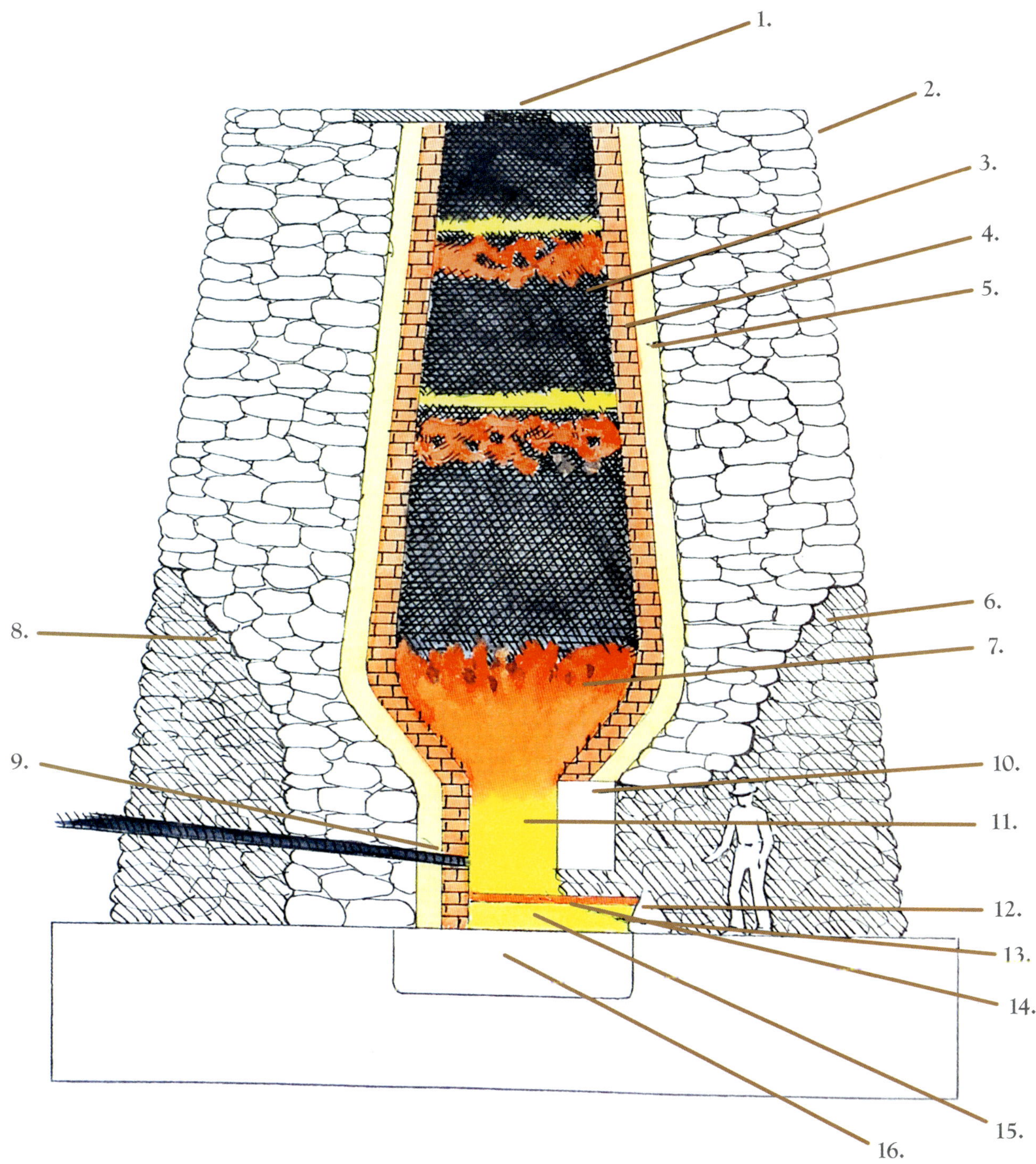

The earliest surviving cast iron products in Europe are boundary posts placed in 1345–1361 at a site now in modern Poland.[2] Blast furnaces producing cast iron were operating in Belgium and France by 1340.[3] Initial products were flat castings such as grave slabs and fire backs. Cored castings such as cannon and pots soon followed.

The earliest English furnace of record was at Newbridge in 1496.[4] Pot casting in England had begun by 1543 when a pot was noted sent to Robertsbridge from Buxted where the foundry was located. Pot founding increased through the seventeenth century, although the products remained quite heavy.[5]

For well-to-do households, the preferred material for cooking vessels remained bronze or copper. Even today the wealthy home is liable to harbor a number of copper pots prominently on display. The preponderance of copper-alloy vessels over those of iron surviving from the seventeenth century bears this out.

According to the Frenchman Reaumur, who wrote *Memoirs on Steel and Iron* in 1722,

> "There are three reasons why cast iron utensils of this sort have not been adopted for more general use. (1) They always look dirty. Because they are rough both inside and out, it is not easy to clean them. (2) They are thicker than vessels made of forged copper and for that reason more difficult to heat. (3) Finally, they break easily. It would not be easy for the cook to handle them. They must be treated with care; it is risky to rap upon them sharply."[6]

By the seventeenth century, holloware technology was far enough advanced, with increasing demand among common folk, for John Winthrop Jr., a guiding force behind the establishment of an ironworks in Massachusetts in the 1640s, to focus a portion of its output on pots sold in the surrounding countryside. The original furnace was set up at Braintree in 1645, but was later abandoned in 1647 for a better site at Lynn.[7]

A letter written by ironworks shareholder Robert Childs to John Winthrop Jr., 15 March 1647 says: "We have cast some tuns of pots, likewise mortars, stoves, skillets. Our potter is molding more at Braintree as yet, which place after another blowing we shall quit, not finding mine there."[8]

Discarded waste products from the Lynn (Saugus) furnace are prolific in pot elements, especially ears and the pentagonal leg with widened foot typical of holloware from this earliest successful American blast furnace.[9] These were loam-molded castings, the technology in use prior to 1707 when Abraham Darby patented the sand-casting in flasks method that would be used into modern times (refer to the loam molding process described in the copper and bronze section).

John Winthrop Jr. established the first American blast furnaces in Massachusetts during the 1640s to cast iron vessels.

Abraham Darby was granted a patent in 1707 that revolutionized the making of cast iron holloware.

In 1707 Abraham Darby, an ironmaster of Coalbrookdale, Shropshire, England, was granted a patent for,

> "A NEW WAY OF CASTING IRON BELLIED POTS, AND OTHER IRON BELLIED WARE IN SAND ONLY, WITHOUT LOAM OR CLAY, BY WHICH IRON POTS, AND OTHER WARE MAY BE CAST FINE AND WITH MORE EASE AND EXPEDITION, AND MAY BE AFFORDED CHEAPER THAN THEY CAN BE BY THE WAY COMMONLY USED, AND IN REGARD TO THEIR CHEAPNESS MAY BE OF GREAT ADVANTAGE TO THE POORE OF THIS OUR KINGDOM, WHO FOR THE MOST PART USE SUCH WARE, AND IN ALL PROBABILITY WILL PREVENT THE MERCHANTS OF ENGLAND GOING TO FOREIGN MARKETS FOR SUCH WARE, FROM WHENCE GREAT QUANTITIES ARE IMPORTED..."[10]

This patent marked a major change in the way vessels were cast. From this date, the loam-molding method was used less and less, although there may have been European foundries employing it as late as the mid-eighteenth century.[11] The new technology, casting cored holloware in a multi-part flask or box filled with adhesive sand would revolutionize the industry. It marks an easily recognized change in manufacture and is a dating milepost.

Darby's exact method was is not spelled out in the patent but it apparently involved a reusable box filled with molding sand. It consisted of three parts—two sides and the top (the actual pot bottom, since pots were cast bottom up). This allowed the vessel to be freed without completely destroying the mold. The use of a pattern of two pot halves around which the sand was packed saved much time previously employed in turning and baking the clay loam mold only to destroy it to remove the pot.

Use of a relatively dry molding sand would prevent the generation of steam during casting, which could disrupt the mold and ruin the cast.[12]

Eighteenth-century casting flasks for pots were called "cheeks" and were made in cylindrical form of cast iron with two halves parting vertically.[13] "Check patterns" are listed in a Coalbrookdale inventory of

1718.[14] A Pine Grove Furnace, Cumberland County, Pennsylvania, "Waste Book" credits molders John Sour and Nicholas Mullen with casting "6 pair cheeks" each in August of 1786.[15]

In use, the two halves were placed on a bottom board and a third section, which could be lifted off, surmounted them. The procedure was as follows:

1. The pot pattern (the pot body minus ears and legs) in halves was placed bottom up on a board.

2. Holes in the pattern received pins used to fix the position of the ear pieces (two each), which were then applied. Marks made by these pins are often found inside the sloping rim where the ear joins and at the outer base of the ear.

3. The two cheek pieces of cast iron hooked together were set around the pattern, which was dusted with finely ground charcoal. The charcoal dust insured that the mold and pattern would separate neatly. It also gave the finished vessel a smooth surface. The cheeks were then filled with molding sand tamped firm.

4. The third section of the mold, a complete cylinder of narrow height the same diameter as the assembled cheeks was set on top. This encompassed the pot bottom. Patterns for legs and gate or sprue were set in place as it was packed with sand. The mouth was filled to the top with sand and shaved level.

5. A board was placed over the mold and the whole assembly was turned over exposing the pot interior which was dusted and packed with sand.

6. The mold was turned once more so as to be "bottom up" and the upper casing comprising the pot bottom was removed. Leg patterns were pulled from it.

7. The two side cheeks were removed leaving the body pattern clear. Ear and body patterns were removed.

8. Next the surfaces were dusted with powdered charcoal and rubbed smooth. This gave the finished vessel a shiny, smooth surface.

9. The two outer halves and bottom were re-assembled and tightly fastened.

10. The gate or sprue was prepared by removing its pattern and rounding off sharp edges of the hole. The mold was then ready to be poured.

An expert could mold a large pot in about twenty minutes. Apprentices, usually young boys, were trained by molding smaller sizes. As a result, small pots and kettles are often found to have crooked ears, misplaced legs, or other minor defects.[16]

This technology quickly supplanted the cumbersome baked-loam method during the 1720s. By 1732, it was used in America. In that year, William Byrd of Virginia described various aspects of ironmaking as practiced at the works of Governor Spotswood. At the Massaponax foundry Spotswood used an air or reverberatory furnace to remelt pig iron from his blast furnace and cast it into household utensils, including pots. The air furnace refined pig iron by melting it free of contact with the fuel. By 1717, in England, Darby was using this method to cast thinner pots.[17] Most pots were cast via iron ladled directly from the blast furnace. Smaller, finer pieces where thinner castings were required utilized the air furnace, a refinement of foundry technology unusual in eighteenth century America.

Spotswood showed Byrd his general operation, but his molder would not reveal complete details of the process. Byrd wrote: "The potter (molder) was so complaisant as to show me the whole process, for which I paid him and the other workmen my respects in the most agreeable way. There was a great deal of ingenuity in the framing of the moulds, wherein they cast the several utensils, but without breaking them to pieces, I found there was no being let into that secret."[18]

Darby's method for casting pots was in use in America by 1720–1730. This method, with some minor changes, has remained in use to the present day.

At about the same time in New England, Joseph Mallinson owned a furnace in Duxbury, Massachusetts. In 1739, he petitioned the government for a grant of land in recognition of the great benefit he had provided to the community as the sole promoter of holloware made in sand molds. He claimed the province could save £20,000 by not importing pots.[19] The same technology was ascribed to Jeremy Florio of Kingston, Massachusetts prior to 1755.[20] Both were located in what is now Plymouth County, in an area where there were eight furnaces casting holloware from bog iron skimmed from ponds, between 1735 and 1835. Bog ore, high in phosphorus, is formed by the precipitation of iron in ground water with the aid of certain bacteria. Left alone for twenty years or more, this iron oxide could form ore containing up to fifty-three percent iron to be scooped from the bottom of bogs.[21]

In Pennsylvania, William Branson, Philadelphia merchant and furnace owner advertised, "Very good iron pots and kettles, fine and light" in July of 1731. These were undoubtedly cast at a furnace in Coventryville, Pennsylvania, built about 1722 that he co-owned with Samuel Nutt.[22] The terms "fine and light" indicate a desire to compete with the English products being sold by that time in large numbers from Abraham Darby's Coalbrookdale works. It seems certain that Darby's sand-casting method reached these shores by 1720, despite efforts to keep it secret. Sand casting was certainly in use by 1730 in Massachusetts, Virginia, and Pennsylvania.

American pots, except for a few seventeenth century vessels possibly cast at Saugus or New Haven, will be of the Darby type, formed in a three-part mold.

After 1707, whether a pot was cast utilizing a sprue or gate is not an indicator of age, but reflects the preference of the founder. Changes in the form of the ears on holloware are the more reliable indicator of age. Ears changed in shape from angular to fully curved over a one hundred year span.

After the demise of the furnaces at Braintree, Saugus, and New Haven in the late seventeenth century, no new furnaces were successful until the 1720s in America. American pots, except for a few possibly seventeenth century vessels cast at Saugus or New Haven, will be of the Darby type, formed in a three-part mold.

This sand-casting method of molding pots was in use in some cases until 1900. It was simplified in some foundries about 1840 by molds of two halves divided vertically through the ears, with half of the ear being a part of each pattern half. The three-part Darby method is recognized by the parting line of the top of the flask (but bottom of the pot) running around the base of the pot, as well as two vertical lines extending from the bottom line to the rim on opposite sides midway between the ears. (See page 39.) Molten iron was dipped from the furnace hearth in an iron ladle lined with clay and carried to the mold. The opening through which the iron was poured into the mold was called a sprue if round or a gate if an elongated slot. The pattern for a sprue was a tapered pin while that of a gate was an elongated wedge.[23] Both made larger openings at the surface than at the inner cavity that would fill with iron to become a pot.

Sprues are typically seen more often on English pots than American examples. Those made at Coalbrookdale may have used baked loam cores.[24] The gate also appears on pots with Darby's molding method and was used starting in 1707. Whether a molder used a sprue or a gate appears to have been a matter of choice.

Some pots have a gate mark over an apparent sprue. This indicates that a pot cast with a sprue was filed in half and used as a pattern for a new pot cast via a gate. (See page 36.) While a sprue is the mark of an earlier pot, for a pre-Darby example, it is what one would expect to find. However, it is not an indicator of age after 1707, though found often on earlier examples of the three-piece mold type, especially those of English origin.

A better indicator of approximate age of an iron pot is the form of the ears, the lugs for bail attachment which project from the rim near the top and extend out and then down to join the pot body at the shoulder. The vertical ear piece changes in cross-section from round to triangular and in outline from angular to curved. There are many subtle variations and changes which will be best understood by noting the progression of ears chronologically through the vessels in this study. When assigning a date to a pot, note the form, seams which identify the casting technique, shape and cross-section (section) of the ears, and shape and section of the legs. The latest feature will be closest to the date, despite others that may look early. When assessing ears, remember that a furnace or foundry would use a pattern until it wore out, then replace it with a new one, which was often in a later style. Consequently, changes in one feature may span a number of years. The changes of form and ears in the charts should be taken only as general guides to dates.

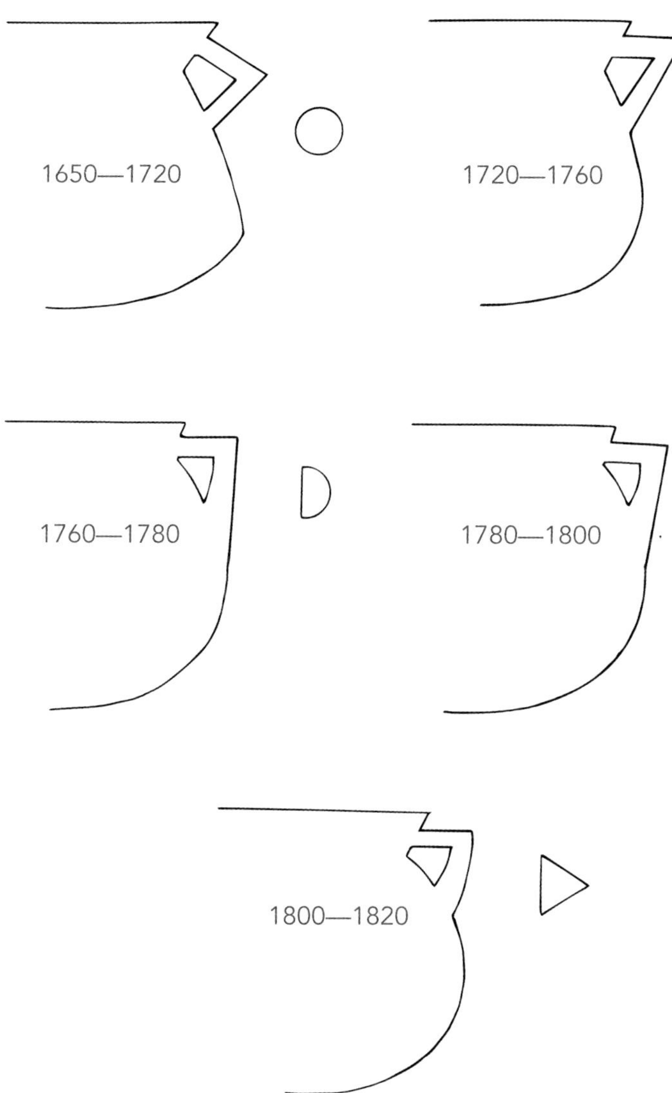

In general, the angular ears of round section with no widening at the shoulder are early seventeenth century to mid-eighteenth century. However, examination of casting parts broken and rejected at the Saugus ironworks revealed some of the curved down to the shoulder type typical of the nineteenth century. The section extending out from the rim, on which the bail pivots, typically angled down on earlier pots in a pronounced way, but by 1750 most extended out horizontally. Some early ears with a curved vertical section also have horizontal top pieces.

Ear patterns were of two pieces. The joint where they meet on the earliest of the curved sort was formed by a tenon on the horizontal piece passing through a hole in the vertical leg. On early, angular types, the horizontal piece rests in a notch at the upper end of the vertical section. Later types rest the top piece on the vertical piece or butt against it. Eighteenth-century French pots and kettles have curved ears with the top piece extending over the curved vertical part. They are round in section with little or no taper.

During the second half of the eighteenth century, the vertical ear piece, still round in section, gradually widened where it meets the pot shoulder. By 1790, it was beginning to exhibit a rounded triangular section with the point on its outer face. As time went on, this triangular section became more pronounced, with sharply defined edges and an inward curve to the inner face of the vertical ear piece. This change appears to date to 1780–1810. By 1810 both inner and outer faces of the vertical piece curved gently in to the pot shoulder. By 1820–1830, at the end of the years when holloware was cast at the blast furnace directly from the molten metal, the ear was very wide at the shoulder with a very pronounced curve. From 1830 on, most holloware was cast at foundries where cast iron pigs or scrap was broken up and remelted for casting into pots, kettles, and other cast iron finished products. This remelting resulted in a more refined metal, which could be cast thinner with a smoother surface than previously. During this period, 1830–1900, many ears were of a single-piece pattern, curved like a cow's horn tapering to the rim from the shoulder. Patterns for these were easier to withdraw from the mold prior to casting and are the final ear form. They were replaced about 1900 by simple horizontal tab extensions from the rim with holes for a bail, usually wire by this time, to pass through. These changes occurred at different times among various furnaces and foundries and should be taken as a broad, general guide for pot dating.

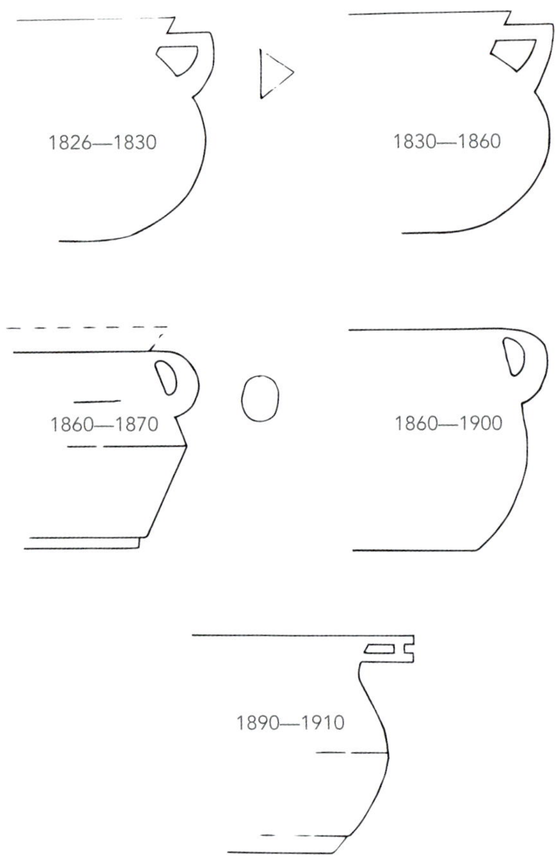

Legs and feet also exhibit some changes indicative of date. Seventeenth century legs are usually faceted with five or six sides with a widening at the bottom into a foot. Those found in the rejects at Saugus are of the five-sided with widening foot sort and appear to be an identifying feature of Saugus holloware, though it is possible they were used in other places. (See page 69.)

Changes in legs and feet over time are also indicators of date. Forms changed from faceted with pronounced feet, to D section, to triangular section, and then to round, as well as from long to stubs, and heavy to light.

Holloware patterns were among the most valuable assets of a furnace or foundry.

Early Darby products may have legs that are merely triangular stumps an inch or so long for a pot of one gallon or less. These resemble legs on Dutch bronze pots with which Darby was familiar. Usually a pot will have longer legs. Eighteenth and early nineteenth-century French pots and kettles continued to have molded or faceted legs and pronounced feet. Mid-eighteenth century legs tend to be heavy and thick; later legs became progressively lighter and shorter.

In section, most eighteenth and early nineteenth century legs are D shaped with the flat surface positioned inward. Nineteenth-century legs were often of triangular section, positioned with a flat surface inward. Some are widely splayed while others, such as those on wares from Pine Grove Furnace, Cumberland County, Pennsylvania, are set well under the body of the pot in an almost vertical position. Legs set well under and having a wide splay are typical of the nineteenth century. Frequently, legs have been eroded by hearth fires so as to resemble a tapered leg widening out into a hoof. These can be deceptive, especially if all three legs are evenly worn. (See page 35, top.)

By the 1830–1850 period, pots made for use on stoves had vestigial legs that were mere stubs. Pots made to be hung over open fires continued to have longer legs. Often large pots and kettles used for washing, butchering, lard rendering, and the like have once longer legs eroded to stumps that may look to be the original length but are not. (See page 54, bottom.)

Patterns for early holloware were among the most valuable assets held by blast furnace operators. They were made of wood (the least desirable since they wore out quickly and were subject to warping), iron, pewter, or brass. Brass patterns were the most desirable and of the highest value.

The mold room at the New Furnace at Darby's Coalbrookdale ironworks in 1718 contained brass pot patterns. A large fifteen gallon pattern set was valued at £10, a large sum at that time when a workman might not make as much in a year.[25] Other patterns were of iron and valued at a fraction of those of brass. Check (cheek) patterns, the two halves of the iron cylinders in which pots were cast, were valued at £1. The basic set of pot patterns included two sides, four ear pieces, and three legs–nine in all.[26]

Letters of Edward Burd of Philadelphia, Pennsylvania, to Jasper Yeats of Lancaster, Pennsylvania, in 1786 discussed pot patterns. His remarks pointed out the problems of wood patterns and those of iron.

April 8, 1786, Edward wrote: "I have been inquiring about pot patterns. It is said they are not permitted to be sent from England now that ye Potts Family had taken English pots and made them serve as moulds, which made their pots too heavy and clumsy. Mr. Wall says this man can make wooden patterns. Mr. Baker says they may serve once and if they are made very thin, you might cast pots thin enough to serve as patterns, but the wooden patterns will not last long because they will warp. He says Mr. Rutter is going to have Pewter Patterns, which may be hardened as much as brass, and will let me know if the thing takes effect."

October 13, 1786: "Col. Cox says he has ye only brass pot moulds in America; they cost him £300; he has them from one to twelve gallons, and would not take £1000 for them. He says if we would get wooden moulds made out of Laurel Root or Mahogany and cast a mould in iron, it would do; as Laurel Root and Mahogany, take ye best polish. If not you must take some of his pots as patterns and file them in two. Perhaps on our situation it would be ye best plan to do so; some other furnaces have done it."[27]

Colonel Cox of the second letter was probably John Cox , a former owner of Batsto Furnace in New Jersey.[28] That pot patterns were valued items of an ironworkers inventory is apparent by their mention in auction notices and sale bills. At a meeting in 1765 of the owners of the Carlisle Ironworks, situated at Boiling Springs, Pennsylvania, pot, kettle, and skillet patterns were noted on hand to mold holloware.[29] Pot patterns as well as stove patterns were listed at the bankruptcy sale of Martic Furnace, Lancaster County, Pennsylvania, in 1769.[30] At Mt. Pleasant Furnace, Berks County, Pennsylvania, November 16, 1796: "With the premises will also be sold or let a number of flasks, patterns, etc."[31]

An inventory of the estate of Isaac Zane, owner of Marlboro Furnace near Winchester, Virginia, taken prior to his death in 1795 lists 413 pounds of pewter patterns. Included were several sizes of pots, kettles, and Dutch ovens, as well as skillets and mortars. Zane had gone to considerable expense to acquire these patterns, which would not shrink or warp "out of round" as wooden ones did.[32]

At the Pine Grove furnace in July 1786 Michael Bush was credited with molding pot patterns of two and eight gallon sizes.[33] On July 12, 1825, Andrew Bombash molded twenty-two patterns of various kinds for $5 at the same furnace.[34] The molding of pot patterns, which would then be cast in iron and used themselves as molding patterns, used a previously cast pot filed in half with ears and legs removed as a pattern. Perhaps a wooden pattern made by a skilled pattern maker would be used. One such artisan who did work for Pine Grove was Joseph R. Henry of Abbotstown, Pennsylvania, 1793–1869.[35] He was listed on the November 1825 tax assessment for Berwick Township of Adams County, Pennsylvania, as a "stove and hollowware pattern maker."[36]

By this time the casting of hollowware at blast furnaces started to be phased out. Pine Grove furnace probably cast few pots after 1830 when Laurel Forge near Pine Grove Furnace was built to refine cast iron pigs into wrought iron blooms. Furnace production then turned mainly to pig iron for the forge.[37]

Others continued holloware production into the 1840s. The two Hampton Furnaces in the Perkiomen Valley of Pennsylvania purchased pot and kettle patterns worth $60.25 between 1836 and 1841.[38]

By the 1830s, most holloware production was taken over by foundries. The foundry using a cupola furnace, powered by a steam engine, could be located in a town or village handy to railroads and commerce. Here cast pigs from a blast furnace and scrap iron were remelted to produce a myriad of cast items. This further refining of the iron allowed it to be cast into more intricate items with a much finer, smoother finish. Pots and kettles were made thinner and lighter than those cast directly from the furnace. Many foundries employed their own pattern makers, unlike the furnaces, which hired traveling artisans for a period of time or purchased from one in their area, as Pine Grove did from Joseph Henry.

The bails or arched handles for the pots and kettles were forged from wrought iron rods by blacksmiths employed by the furnace or foundry.

The use of the cupola furnace, powered by steam or electricity, to remelt scrap or pig iron removed holloware production from the blast furnace to the foundry about 1830.

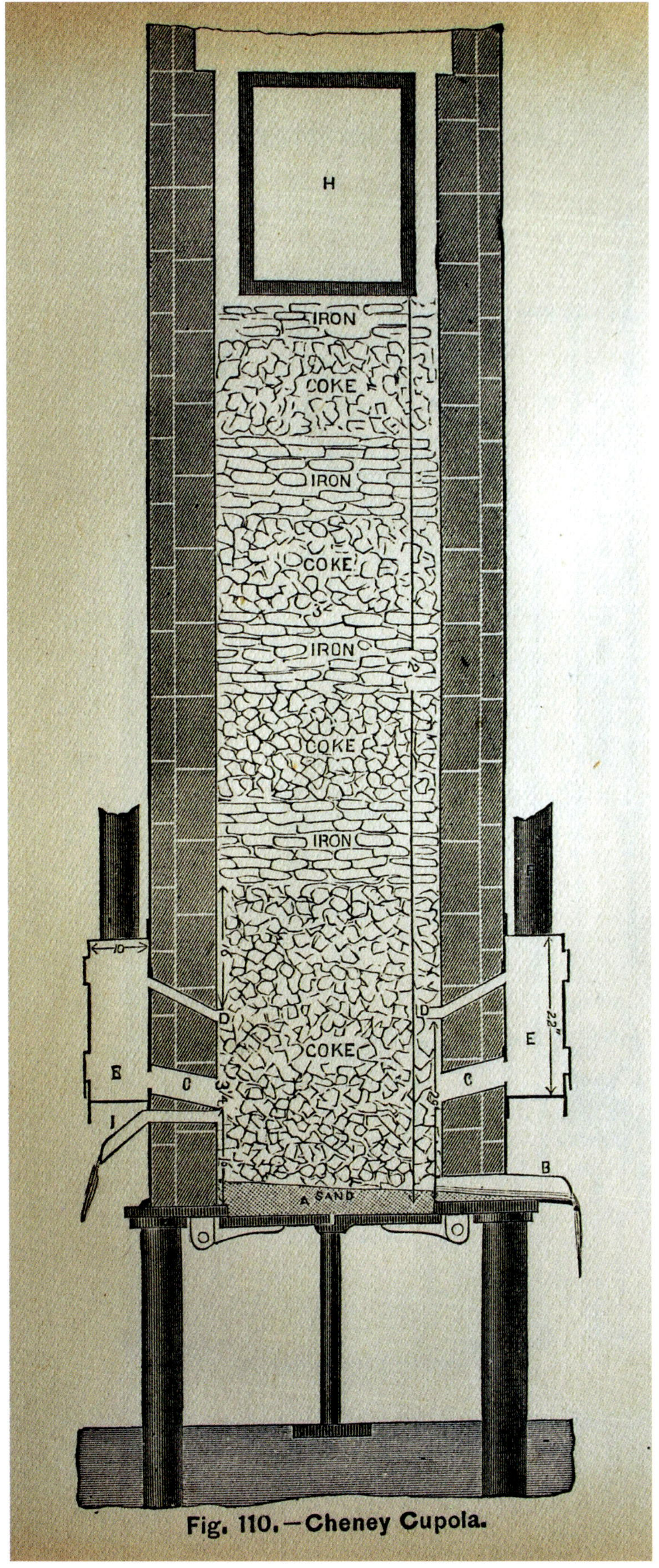

Eighteenth century bails are often heavy and forged down to a smaller dimension where they were curved to swivel through the pot ear. Some terminated in a tiny curl.

Often the seventeenth century bails were flattened where they fit around the top section of the ear. Some furnace blacksmiths produced distinctive bails, those from Pine Grove being heavier than normal. By 1830–1850 most bails were made of heavy gauge wire of 3/16 inch to 1/4 inch diameter and by 1900 used 1/8 inch diameter wire needing no forging to bend and shape it.

Changing forms are the basis for many of the dates assigned to holloware in this study. Only in rare instances were pots, kettles, or teakettles marked as to maker or place prior to the mid-nineteenth century. Dated examples are even more unusual. Marked vessels thus become points on a timeline to deduce approximate dates of the unmarked. Similarly, place names, furnace names, plus owner's and merchant's initials may help to relate a form to a geographic area. Wherever a vessel is documented by a specific reference, this will be noted.

Cupola Furnace, ca. 1880, height 12′ above bed plate, diameter 48″. A. Sand bottom, B. Iron runner, C. Lower Tuyere, D. Upper Tuyere, E. Wind chamber, F. Blast pipe, H. Charging door, I. Slag runner. Firebrick lined metal sheathed cylinder is filled (charged) with alternate layers of coke and iron. The furnace sits on metal columns so the bottom may be dropped for cleaning and brick renewal. The air blast is powered by a steam engine or an electric motor (1900). From *The Moulder's Textbook etc.* by Thomas D. West, 1885.

Pot Identification

To identify a pot, note whether its form is rounded, angular sided, or squashed, etc., and the style and cross-section of the ears. Compare with the form and ear chart (see page 25 & 26) to estimate a range of dates, then examine the examples in that range to find the closest match.

Features changed at different times among the various furnaces and foundries. Patterns for ears were made of wood and wore out before metal body patterns, hence they are the best guide to a date. Conversely, pot body patterns, often made of another iron pot minus the ears and legs, cut in half, lasted a long time. Therefore pot forms between 1770 and 1830 show little, if any, change.

The latest feature will date the pot, even if others appear to be earlier. After 1840, many pots were cast in molds of two halves parting vertically through the ears. Half of each ear was thus a part of each mold half. Some of these ears were very angular and of a much earlier style. In this case, the two-part mold separating through the ears is the latest date-determining feature, not the ear. (See page 50, bottom.)

Note that eighteenth century legs are usually of D section while nineteenth century legs are generally of a triangular section. Later legs are lighter and often have hollowed backs. Transitional legs (1780–1820) are D section tending into triangular, with each side slightly rounded. Examine these and other details closely. Many changes giving clues to dates are minor.

Early illustrations, rather than written descriptions, are vital elements of reference. Early woodcut prints, for instance those found in books printed in New England, show a type of pot where the body is drawn in at the shoulder so that the slanting rim diameter is visibly less than that of the bellied section. This is a New England form typical of the first half of the eighteenth century. (See page 34.) By the 1850s, forms were becoming standardized. Major iron foundries in cities and minor ones in country towns produced vessels essentially alike. This was also the era in which the cook stove replaced the open hearth fire as a cooking medium. Pots and kettles reflected this change with stubby feet, simple shapes, and the inset or "pit" bottom, which could be set inside a round hole on the stove top.

Foreign cast iron vessels noted in this study are usually from Britain or Scotland, Spain and Portugal, or France—all have distinctive forms. In addition to forms as clues to geographic origin, they can also be indicators of date. In some instances variations are subtle, in others less so.

In general terms, seventeenth-century pots had very slightly curved sides sloping to a sharply angular curve under to the bottom. (See page 30.) They tended to have wide flanged rims. Early eighteenth century examples from about 1730 to 1750 retained this shape, but by 1750 the body became more rounded. (See page 37.) About 1830 to 1840 the form became more squashed-rounded but compressed. (See page 48.) Then came the cook stove and pots more like cylinders with a slight bulge to the sides. (See page 55.) A variation of the cylinder form was the "Dutch Pot," having slightly concave sides tapering in to the rim, which had an inset ledge to take a fitted lid. These were originally a seventeenth century Low Countries product, perhaps imported by Dutch in the Hudson Valley, New York, or Hartford, Connecticut, area and later cast at Saugus or New Haven. Eighteenth century examples lost the concave sides. The form persisted until about 1830. (See page 65.)

TOP to BOTTOM:

Pot, cast iron, wrought iron, American, ca. 1646. Height 4.5", rim diameter 4.5". Seventeenth century slope-sided form with deep belly and down-sloping-angular ears. Traditionally known as the first casting made at the Hammersmith Ironworks at Saugus, Massachusetts. This small pot descended in the family of Thomas Hudson, who obtained it immediately after it was cast.[39] *Courtesy of the Lynn Public Library, Lynn, Massachusetts.*

Cast in a two-part, baked-loam mold evidenced by the parting seam passing from rim to rim under the pot body. Atypical (for Saugus) D section legs are worn to one half original length. Sprue worn away. *Courtesy of the Lynn Public Library, Lynn, Massachusetts.*

LEFT to RIGHT:

Pot, cast iron, steel, American, ca. 1720–1765. Height 7.5", rim diameter 7.5". Possibly cast in Pennsylvania or Virginia. Early slope-sided form with down-sloping-angular ears of round section. Cast in a three-part mold. Replaced steel bail.

The pot has a gate on the bottom and D section legs worn to stumps.

Pot, cast iron, wrought iron, American, ca. 1720–1765. Height 10.75", rim diameter 11.5". Angular down-turned ears and early deep-bellied form. Three-part mould with large gate. D section legs. A larger version of the previous pot, probably cast at the same furnace. Original wrought iron bail.

LEFT to RIGHT:

Pot, cast iron, steel, American, probably Plymouth County, Massachusetts, ca. 1720–1740. Height 12", rim diameter 13.875". Large cauldron size with straight-sloped early form. Wide lip typical of early pots, angular ears, three-part mould. Steel replaced bail.

D section legs eroded to stumps. Cast using two gates.

Early postcard showing a loam-molded cauldron of English form that belonged to the Pilgrim Miles Standish. Note its similarity to the above pot. It is part of the collections of Pilgrim Hall, Plymouth, Massachusetts.

Pot, cast iron, wrought iron, American, ca. 1720–1750. Height 7.75", rim diameter 6.75", belly diameter 8.75". The New England form with a deep curve from the side into the lip. Three-part mold. Angular ears, round in section, widened slightly at the shoulder. D section legs with wide splay eroded to stumps. Original early square section, wrought iron bail.

Pots, cast iron, wrought iron, American, ca. 1730–1750. Height 5", rim diameter 4", and height 10.5", rim diameter 10". These pots exemplify the early New England form.

Pot, cast iron, wrought iron, American, ca. 1730–1760. Height 11.5", rim diameter 11". New England form, angular ears, heavy D section legs, three-part mold. Two gates for two casters pouring simultaneously to insure uniform filling of large mold. Original wrought iron bail.

Pot, cast iron, wrought iron, American, ca. 1750–1760. Height 11.25", rim diameter 11.75". A later New England form showing a less pronounced curve to the rim than earlier examples. Heavy D section legs with wide splay. Three-part mold with single thick gate. Original wrought iron bail, angular round-section ears.

Pot, cast iron, wrought iron, American, ca. 1750–1770. Height 9,5", rim diameter 10". A later New England form. Three-part mold with gate. D section, fire-eroded legs show how erosion gives the mistaken conception of a hoof or foot.

Pot, cast iron, wrought iron, American, ca. 1790–1810. Height 10.5", rim diameter 11.25". Rounded form with angular ears of round section widened at shoulder. Three-part mold. Lightweight D section tapering legs. Gate on bottom. Old, but not original, bail.

Marked "ELLIS GRIFFETH" in a rectangular cartouche on the shoulder. Probably cast at a Carver, Massachusetts, furnace. Ellis Griffeth was a Carver resident in the late eighteenth and early nineteenth centuries.[40]

Pot, cast iron, wrought iron, English, ca. 1720–1750. Height 5.5", rim diameter 6". A casting from coke-smelted iron of a rounded form with a narrow rim, which is apparently English.[41] Small, round-section, angular ears, unusual astragal-molded cordons. Three-part mold. Original wrought iron, square-section bail.

Heavy gate over a sprue mark from an original pot cut in half and used as a pattern. D section fire-eroded legs may have been much longer originally. This may be a Darby, Coalbrookdale pot.

Pot, cast iron, steel, English, ca. 1750–1760. Height 7.75", rim diameter 7.25". Full-rounded English form with a narrow lip. Three-part mold with a gate. Angular, round-section ears widened at the shoulder, D section legs, replaced steel bail.

Pot, cast iron, steel, English, ca. 1750–1760. Height 5.5", rim diameter 6". Rounded English form with a narrow lip. Three-part mold with gate. Angular, round-section ears widened at the shoulder. D section legs, replaced bail.[42]

Pots, cast iron, wrought iron, American, ca. 1760–1780. Height 7″, rim diameter 7″, and height 14″, rim diameter 15.5″. These pots may have been cast at either the Hampton Furnace near Emmitsburg or Antietam Furnace near Hagerstown, Maryland. The flared out ears are typical of Antietam furnace.[43] Original wrought iron bails.

Both pots are cast with three-piece molds. The large pot has a sprue on the bottom and legs eroded to stumps.

The Antietam Furnace was small, twelve feet square at the base.[44] It may have been difficult to achieve optimum casting conditions as evidenced by several copper rivets plugging holes in the vessel where the wall was porous.

Pot, cast iron, wrought iron, tin, American, ca. 1760–1780. Height 6.625", rim diameter 5.25". Round form with narrow lip, similar to English form. Three-part mold with thick gate. Original wrought iron bail. D section legs. The smooth surface texture, typical of charcoal-smelted iron, suggests this vessel is American rather than English. Tin lid may be original.

D section ears flat on the back, widened to the shoulder. The ear now begins to change from the round-section type to one tending towards the triangular. Ear pattern pin is evident on the lower part of the ear.

Pot, cast iron, wrought iron, American, ca. 1760–1770. Height 8.5", rim diameter 7.75". Three-part mold with gate. Triangular-section legs. Original wrought iron bail.

Rounded triangular-section ears that are flat on the inside and widening out to the pot shoulder in straight lines indicate a change from the angular round-section earlier ear to a new type that will remain triangular in section as it begins to gently curve into the shoulder.

Pot, cast iron, wrought iron, American, ca. 1781–1782. Height 8.75", rim diameter 9". This somewhat less than fully rounded form will prevail until about 1830. Three-part mold with gate. Triangular-section ear with straight outer edge and slight curve to inner surface. Legs triangular in section. Original wrought iron bail.

Pot, cast iron, wrought iron, American, ca. 1781–1782. Height 12", rim diameter 13.5". Rounded shallow-belly form marked "PINE GROVE" on shoulder. Three-part mold with gate. Original wrought iron bail.

Triangular-section ears straight on the outer edge but with a slight inward curve.

Triangular-section legs set well under with little splay and with a step or fillet where they join the body were typical of Pine Grove products.

Pine Grove Furnace, Cumberland County, Pennsylvania, began operations 1781 and cast pots into the 1830s. It ceased operation in 1895.[45]

Pot, cast iron, wrought iron, American, ca. 1781–1790. Height 9", rim diameter 8.875". Rounded shallow-belly form. Three-part mold with gate. Triangular-section ears curved inside and out. Has Pine Grove characteristics of triangular-section legs with step, legs set well under, heavy original bail, and two cordons at the base of the ear.

Pot, cast iron, wrought iron, American, ca. 1790–1810. Height 9", rim diameter 8.5". Shallow-belly form. Three-part mold with gate. Triangular-section ears and legs. Original wrought iron bail. Upturned ear is the result of the use of incorrect ear patterns intended for the straight sides of a kettle or Dutch oven.

Lid, cast iron, ca. 1830–1840. Later cast lids with ledged rims intended for kettles or Dutch ovens are sometimes matched to pots. Original pot lids were usually tin or sheet iron, flat with wrought iron or tin handles.

Pot, cast iron, wrought iron, American, ca. 1790. Height 10.5", rim diameter 12". From Fayette County, Pennsylvania, possibly cast at Alliance Furnace. Shallow-belly form, three-part mold with a gate. Rectangular-section ears, slightly curved outside, curved and widened inside. Heavy triangular-section legs, original wrought iron bail.

Pot, cast iron, wrought iron, American, ca. 1800–1810. Height 6.75", rim diameter 5.75". Shallow-belly form, three-part mold with gate. Short triangular-section ear with pronounced inner curve typical of 1800–1810. Triangular-section legs, original wrought iron bail. Tin lid may be original.

Ear patterns intended for kettles or Dutch ovens having straight sides had longer vertical sections than those intended for pots, where the ear only extended to the shoulder. When used to cast a pot, this longer vertical section resulted in an upturned ear.

CLOCKWISE:

Pot, cast iron, wrought iron, American, ca. 1800–1810. Height 6.25", rim diameter 7". Shallow-belly form, three-part mold with gate. This may be a Pine Grove pot. Cleaned to bare metal.

Triangular-section short ears with inner curves have steps where they join the pot body. Original wrought iron bail has forged rat tail curls where it circles the ear, an unusual feature.

Triangular-section legs have steps where they join the pot body.

Pot, cast iron, wrought iron, American, ca. 1820–1830. Height 9", rim diameter 8.75". Shallow-belly form, possibly from Pine Grove Furnace, Pennsylvania. Three-part mold with gate. Triangular-section legs and ears with inner and outer ear surfaces curved. Original wrought iron bail. Incorrect (kettle) ear pattern was used.

Pot, cast iron, steel, American, ca. 1830–1835. Height 6", rim diameter 5.5". Shallow-belly form, three-part mold with gate. Triangular-section legs. Replaced steel bail. Probably a Pine Grove pot.

Curved triangular-section ears with a slight reverse curve at the pot shoulder. This curve becomes more pronounced in the 1840–1860 period. Kettle ear patterns were used, hence the dip into the lip.

Pot, cast iron, wrought iron, American, ca. 1830–1835. Height 8.75", rim diameter 8.5". Shallow-belly form, three-part mold with gate. Triangular-section legs and ears. Both inner and outer ear surfaces are now strongly curved in with a reverse curve at the base. Original wrought iron bail.

Pot, cast iron, wrought iron, American, ca. 1830–1850. Height 9", rim diameter 9.5". The squashed-body form crudely executed. Three-part mold with sprue (probably by molder's preference rather than a gate). Round-section ears curved and wide at the shoulder. Original wrought iron bail. Heavy weight and lack of refinement suggest that this is a late country furnace product.

Pot, cast iron, wrought iron, tin, English, ca. 1830. Height 5.875", rim diameter 6.75". A more squashed form typical of 1830–1850, with short triangular-section splayed legs of original length. Curved triangular-section ears. Three-part mold with gate. Original wrought iron wire bail with flattened end loops. Tin lid.

Pot, cast iron, wrought iron, American, ca. 1836–1850. Height 6", rim diameter 5.75". The squashed form with earlier style angular ears. Three-part mold with a gate. Light D section legs, original wrought iron bail.

Marked "AGAWAM 10". The Agawam foundry was established in 1836 at Wareham, Plymouth County, Massachusetts, and was still in operation in 1867.[46] This is a very light, smooth casting typical of nineteenth century foundry work.

Pot, cast iron, wrought iron, American, ca. 1840–1860. Height 5.75", rim diameter 6.25". Squashed form with nearly straight sloping sides. Three-part mold with a thin gate. Reverse-curved ears typical of 1830–1860. Original wrought iron bail. This pot came from the Baltimore, Maryland, area.

Triangular-section legs with hollowed backs set well under are typical of the mid-nineteenth century, as is the long, thin gate.

Marked "CRESSON & CO No.2 4 Qts". William P. Cresson ran a foundry in Philadelphia, Pennsylvania, from before 1849 to his retirement in 1859.[47]

Pot, cast iron, wrought iron, American, ca. 1850. Height 7.375", rim diameter 7.5". Squashed form. Two-part mold parted vertically through the ears with gate. Original wrought iron bail. Ears of triangular section curved with a lobed extension down the pot side. Triangular-section legs with concave sides.

Pot, cast iron, wrought iron, American, ca. 1836–1846. Height 6.5", rim diameter 6.75". Squashed form, three-part mold with gate. Oval-section rounded ears, triangular-section legs with a V groove on back. Original wire bail.

Marked "J. SAVERY & SON NEW YORK" in an oval cartouche and "PHOENIX WORKS No. 12" in another on the opposite side. John Savery and son William operated this foundry in Jersey City, New Jersey, with warehouse and offices in New York according to Bishop's *History of Manufactures.*

Pot, cast iron, steel, American, ca. 1839–1869. Height 7.25", rim diameter 7.5". Squashed form, two-part mold divided through ears and cast with a sprue. Oval-section ears straight outside, curved inside. Light triangular-section legs; one leg is divided by the mould line so as to be under an ear in the traditional manner.

Marked "SAVERY & Co. PHILa". Founded by Peleg Savery, John Savery, and Arad Barrows, this firm was a separate business from that in New York.[48]

Pot, cast iron, steel, American, ca. 1839–1869. Height 11.5", rim diameter 12". Squashed form, three-part mold with gate. Triangular-section earlier style ears, D section legs. Replaced steel bail. A light casting, another Savery & Co. product. Savery & Co. sold pots in light and heavy weights and did not provide bails or lids unless requested.[49]

Pot, cast iron, wrought iron, American, ca. 1858. Height 12", rim diameter 14.5". Squashed form cast in two-part mold parted through the lobed triangular-section ears. wrought iron bail. Marked "S P & Co No 9 6 GALLs". Stuart, Peterson & Co. were major holloware makers in Philadelphia, Pennsylvania, in 1858.[50]

Pot, cast iron, steel, American, ca. 1858. Height 10.5", rim diameter 11.5". Heavy casting of squashed form. Three-part mold with gate. Round-section curved ears. Replaced steel bail. Marked "No. 6 3 GALL, NORTH CHASE & NORTH PHILADELPHIA". This firm also made stoves.[51]

Pot, cast iron, steel, American, ca. 1835–1850. Height 9.5", rim diameter 10". Squashed form, deep pit bottom, three-part mould with long, thin gate. Round-section fully-curved cow's horn ear first appears at this time. Bail replaced. Marked on side "4".

Pot, cast iron, wrought iron, American, ca. 1835–1850. Height 10.5", rim diameter 10.75". Squashed form with deep inset pit bottom for stove top use. Curved triangular-section ears, short stub legs. Three-part mold with gate. Original wire bail. Cook stoves were marketed as early as 1815.[52] Franklin Manning of Portland, Maine, illustrated a pot of this type set into a stove top in an advertisement of 1836.[53]

LEFT to RIGHT:

Pot, cast iron, steel, American, ca. 1850–1880. Height 12.25", rim diameter 14". Squashed form, three-part mold. D section fire-eroded legs, steel replaced bail. Cow's horn ear patterns were of one piece, which was easily removed when preparing the mold. Marked "6 GALL".

Gate on slightly raised area to provide added strength.

Pot, cast iron, steel, American, ca. 1860–1890. Height 13.25", rim diameter 16.375". Squashed form, three-part mold parting horizontally under the lip and at the widest part of the body of the pot. Cow's horn ears, triangular-section eroded hollow-back legs. Replaced steel bail. Two gates since this is a large pot. Marked "12" on bottom.

Pot, cast iron, wrought iron, American, ca. 1861–1879. Height 9", rim diameter 9.5". An elongated cylindrical form with bulging sides, the "bulge pot" now begins to replace the classic pot shape. Three-part mold with long, thin gate. Stub legs, cow's horn ears, original wrought iron wire bail.

Marked in an oval cartouche "J A GOEWAY ALBANY, N Y". John A Goeway was a prolific maker of pots and teakettles. They were typical mid- to late nineteenth century thin, smooth, foundry products.[54]

Pot, cast iron, wrought iron, American, ca. 1850–1880. Height 10.5", rim diameter 11.25". Bulge form with offset dimple pit bottom. Curving rather than angular rim typical of 1860–1880. Three-part mold with gate, stub legs, original wire bail, cow's horn ears.

Marked on bottom "S & K 8". Possibly cast by Shalter and Kauffman at the Mount Penn furnace, Reading, Pennsylvania.[55]

Pot, cast iron, wrought iron, American, ca. 1860–1870. Height 9", rim diameter 9". Bulge form with earlier style of ear. Three-part mold with gate. Offset pit bottom, original wrought iron wire bail. A pot of exactly this style is illustrated in the Dover Stamping Co. catalog of 1869.[56]

LEFT to RIGHT:

Pot, cast iron, wrought iron, American, ca. 1860–1875. Height 10.25", rim diameter 11.5". Angular straight-sided form cast in a three-part horizontally parted mold with a gate. Cow's horn ears, pit bottom with stub legs. Original wrought iron wire bail. Tin lid may be original.

Marked on the bottom " C W & C" for Cox, Whitman, and Cox, Philadelphia, Pennsylvania. They were primarily makers of stoves.[57]

Pot, cast iron, wrought iron, American, ca. 1850–1869. Height 5.875", rim diameter 7.5". Low bulge form used until about 1900. Two-part mold with parting line vertically through ears. Original wire bail and tin lid. Marked on side "SAVERY & Co. PHILADA 8P No 7" Many pots of this type are marked "MARIETTA, PA" on the bottom.

Pot, cast iron, wrought iron, American, ca. 1860–1890. Height 10", rim diameter 11.5". Low bulge form parted horizontally at mid-pot, its curved ear and base are cast separately, set into the pot mold, and cast in. Original wrought iron wire bail.

Marked "Marietta PA" on the bottom.

Pot, cast iron, wrought iron, American, ca. 1890. Height 10", rim diameter 11.5". Late bulge form. Three-part horizontally parting mold with gate at rim ground off. Tipping ring on side, original wrought iron wire bail. Ears extend horizontally from the rim. Marked on bottom "ERIE 9". Cast at the Griswold foundry in Erie, Pennsylvania.[58] Dimple-inset bottom with stub legs.

Sauce pot, cast iron, wrought iron, English, ca. 1850–1900. Height 3.5", rim diameter 4", handle 7". Cast in a two-part horizontal-parting mold. Wrought iron tubular handle riveted to a stub cast on the pot. Earlier handles ended in a pad riveted to the pot.

Marked on bottom "IZONS & Co 1 PINT, No 1". Located in West Bromwich, England, this firm produced cooking ware including "three legged iron pots, Spanish, French pots" etc.[59] Holloware made by Izons, Kenrick, and Clark is frequently found in America, to which it was heavily exported.

British Pots

Pots from Britain have been imported since Colonial times. Many of these British pots were made in Scotland. Most have an identifiable squashed shape with a weak, narrow rim. They tend to have very short stubby legs. Beginning in the early eighteenth century, Britain exported great numbers of hollowares around the world, continuing well into the twentieth century.

The Carron Company and the Fallkirk Iron Company, both located at Fallkirk, Scotland, were large exporters, particularly to South Africa, where a demand persisted well into the twentieth century. Izons, Kenrick and Clark were major producers of a wide variety of holloware in the nineteenth century. Abraham Darby's Coalbrookdale Company also marketed pots to America and Europe in the same period. (See pages 60 and 62.)

Pot, cast iron, wrought iron, Scotland, ca. 1760–1770. Height 5", rim diameter 4.75". Squashed form with weak lip and small legs. Three-part mold with sprue, angular ears, restored wrought iron bail. Likely a product of the Carron Ironworks of Fallkirk, Scotland, founded in 1759.[60]

Pot, cast iron, wrought iron, Scotland, ca. 1770–1790. Height 5.5", rim diameter 5.75". Typical squashed Scottish form with a weak lip. Three-part mold with sprue, small D-section legs, slightly curved round-section ears. Marked on shoulder "CARRON". The Carron Company's first furnace went into blast in December of 1760.[61] Pots were among their initial products and continued to be produced into the twentieth century.[62]

Bottom showing sprue and D section legs.

Pot, cast iron, steel, Scotland, ca. 1820. Height 6.5", rim diameter 8.5". Carron pouched or squashed form with weak lip and short legs set well under. Three-part mold with sprue, curved round-section ears. Replaced steel bail.

Pot, cast iron, steel, probably Scotland, ca. 1830. Height 7.25", rim diameter 8.375". Squashed form. Three-part mold with gate. Ears triangular in section, curved on inner surface, straight on outer surface, short triangular legs. Marked "1" on bottom. Restored steel bail. A very thin, smooth casting, indicating a later date despite earlier type ears.

Pot, cast iron, steel, Scotland, ca. 1830–1870. Height 4.5", rim diameter 5.75". Squashed form, three-part mold with sprue. Round-section ears curved to shoulder, D section legs worn to stumps. Replaced steel bail.

Marked "T- DINGTONS (?) GLasgow".

LEFT to RIGHT:

Pot, cast iron, wrought iron, England, ca. 1870–1890. Height 6.5", rim diameter 7.625". Squashed form, three-part mold with sprue. Round-section curved ears, D-section legs. Original wrought iron bail. Marked "C-B-DAL(E) 1 GALL".

Type of mark and rough finish suggest this is a late product of the Coalbrookdale Company, successors to Abraham Darby.

LEFT to RIGHT:

Pot, cast iron, steel, Scotland, ca. 1890–1930. Height 8.5", rim diameter 9.5". Squashed form, three-part mold with sprue. Round-section curved ears, D section legs. Replaced steel bail.

Marked "2 1/2 GS" on lid. This may be a late product of the Fallkirk Foundry established in 1819.[63] Pot and lid have a rough texture typical of more recent castings.

Lid marked "FALLKIRK Size 3". Pot and lid have grainy texture typical of twentieth-century castings.

Pot, cast iron, steel, South Africa, ca. 1930–1960. Height 10.25", rim diameter 10". Squashed form, two-part mold parting vertically through the ears. Marked on the side "MADE IN SOUTH AFRICA" and "DEFY Size 3". Replaced steel bail.

Bottom with D-shaped legs cast first and inserted into the mold before the body was cast. Gate on rim ground away.

Pot, cast iron, steel, England, ca. 1960–1990. Height 7", rim diameter 8". Squashed form cast in a three-part mold with top halves parting vertically through round-section curved ears. Marked on side "1 GALL" and swan trade mark. Original wire bail.

Bottom showing D section pre-cast legs. Marked "Made in England". Rough, sandy texture.

"Dutch" Pots

A distinctive style of pot was the so-called "Dutch pot" having concave or straight sides inclining in slightly to the top with a rounded bottom and a non-flaring lip to take a fitted lid of cast iron or tin, now usually missing. These were originally a Low Countries form dating back to the sixteenth century. They may have been cast in America at one or all of the three pioneer iron furnaces established by John Winthrop, Jr. in the mid- to late seventeenth century: Braintree and Saugus, Massachusetts, and New Haven, Connecticut. They were possibly marketed to Dutch and Flemish settlers around Long Island Sound and the Hudson River Valley. The New Paltz pot is a prime example. (See below.) A straight-sided version, slanted inward to the rim, was popular in France and was produced until 1830–1835 in America, where it was called a "Dutch Pot." (See page 67.)

Pot, cast iron, wrought iron, American, the Netherlands, or Belgium, ca. 1645–1700. Height 15.75", rim diameter 16.25". A cylindrical, concave-sided Low Countries form called a "Dutch pot" by early American ironworkers.[64] Depicted in Dutch and Belgian genre paintings.[65] Loam molded. Curved ears of round section. Original wrought iron bail. *Courtesy of Historic Huguenot Street, New Paltz, New York.*

Saugus type pentagonal legs with widened out foot suggests a Hammersmith origin. Cast with two sprues and a riser to insure proper filling of the mold. A very heavy casting. *Courtesy of Historic Huguenot Street, New Paltz, New York.*

Pot, cast iron, wrought iron, American (?), ca. 1645–1680. Height 10.5", rim diameter 13.5". Low Countries form cast in a loam mold with five-sided legs eroded to stumps. Ears of flattened triangular section, flat side out with broken curve. Two sprues, original wrought iron bail. This pot strongly resembles a fragment excavated from a Dutch trading post on Burlington Island in the Delaware River near Philadelphia, Pennsylvania.[66]

Horizontal ear piece tenoned through vertical in pattern, an early technique.

Pot, cast iron, wrought iron, French or Belgian, ca. 1750. Height 7.25", rim diameter 9.5". Cylindrical form tapering slightly to the rim, three-part mold with large sprue. Curved round-section ears with horizontal piece overlapping curved section, typical of French castings. Original wrought iron bail. This is the eighteenth century Continental version of the preceding pots.[67]

Bottom showing off-center sprue and faceted six-sided legs eroded to stumps.

Pot, cast iron, wrought iron, American, ca. 1810–1820. Height 11.25", rim diameter 11". Slightly tapering form with hint of concave sides. Three-part mold with gate. Triangular-section ears with curved surfaces. D section legs worn to stubs. Inset rim with wide rise probably for a tin lid. Old replaced wrought iron bail.

Pot, cast iron, wrought iron, American, ca. 1830. Height 10", rim diameter 8.5". Body tapers slightly to top. Three-part mold with a gate. D section angular ears are curved inside and outside with reverse curves at the base. Triangular-section legs with step at top, typical of Pine Grove Furnace, Cumberland County, Pennsylvania. Old replaced bail.

Heavy triangular-section legs set well under with a step at the pot body, typical of Pine Grove Furnace pots.

Spanish Pots

Antique pots of an ancient form have been imported to America from Spain and Portugal in recent years. They are of a bulbous form with long legs and a tall, non-flaring neck. Some retain their original cast iron lids. They range from seventeenth century loam-molded examples (see page 70) to later twentieth century sand castings. Even very late vessels exhibit early features, but casting details mark them as late nineteenth or early twentieth century. (See page 72, top.)

TOP to BOTTOM:

The bottom reveals the mold parting line passing under with no break for a centered sprue, which it would have had if formed on a horizontal rotating lathe-type apparatus. This and the single off-center sprue suggest the molder turned it atop a conventional potter's wheel rotating vertically. African pot casters formed loam molds for large vessels this way in the early twentieth century. *Courtesy Winterthur Museum, Museum purchase.*

Pot, cast iron, wrought iron, probably American, ca. 1644–1670. Height 10.125", diameter 15". This loam-molded pot is attributed to either the Braintree or Saugus, Massachusetts, ironworks based on its pentagonal legs and feet and chemical composition, which matches known Saugus products. Round-section angular ears, replaced wrought iron bail. The unusual form resembles Iberian pots with its high, non-flaring neck. It may have been an attempt to duplicate an early Spanish design. *Courtesy Winterthur Museum, Museum purchase.*

Two Iberian pots, cast iron, wrought iron, ca. 1670–1750.

Pot, cast iron, wrought iron, Iberian, ca. 1670–1730. Height 7.125", rim diameter 4.75". Spanish form with tall, vertical neck. Loam-molded casting with round-section angular ears. Marked "80" on body and lid. Original wrought iron bail with flattened hooks on ends. This form continued to the late nineteenth century. Later pots were parted through the ears.[68]

Sprue on bottom. Tall six-sided legs.

Lid marked "80" with a piece of the lid knocked off to allow the bail to swing up past it.

Pot, cast iron, wrought iron, Iberian, ca. 1720–1750. Height 14.5", rim diameter 7.5". High-neck form cast in three-part mold with large sprue. Lid missing. Angular round-section ears, original twisted wrought iron bail with flattened-end hooks typical of early pots.

Bottom showing large sprue and hollow-back triangular legs having raised moldings on back edges.

Pot, cast iron, steel, Scotland, ca. 1880–1920. Height 10", diameter 9". Cast in a three-part mold with the two halves parting vertically through the ears. D-section, widely splayed legs with slightly hollowed backs. Angular round-section ears of a much earlier style. Gate on the bottom is ground smooth. Original wire bail. Marked on side in an oval "N.°22". White enameled interior. Lid missing. This is a late Spanish style pot probably made at the Falkirk Iron Company in Scotland for export to the Iberian market. Other British foundries, such as Carron and Izons made foreign styles for export as well.

Pot, cast iron, steel, Portugal, ca. 1950. Height 4.75", rim diameter 5.5". Marked "IL" and "Made in Portugal" on bottom. Squashed form cast in a three-part mold parted horizontally with gates on side cordons. Round-section curved ears molded using a two-piece pattern. Original steel wire bail.

Pot, cast iron, steel, probably Chinese, ca. 1950 or later. Height 8.5", rim diameter 9.25". Bulbous form cast in baked-loam three-part mold with vertical parting through the ears. Shrinkage lines on body indicate a baked clay mold. Lid cast with a gate. Ears are rounded, flattened oval in section. Original steel bail with projecting points.

A horizontal parting line on the bottom circles a large, crude sprue. Flattened triangular-section legs are widely splayed.

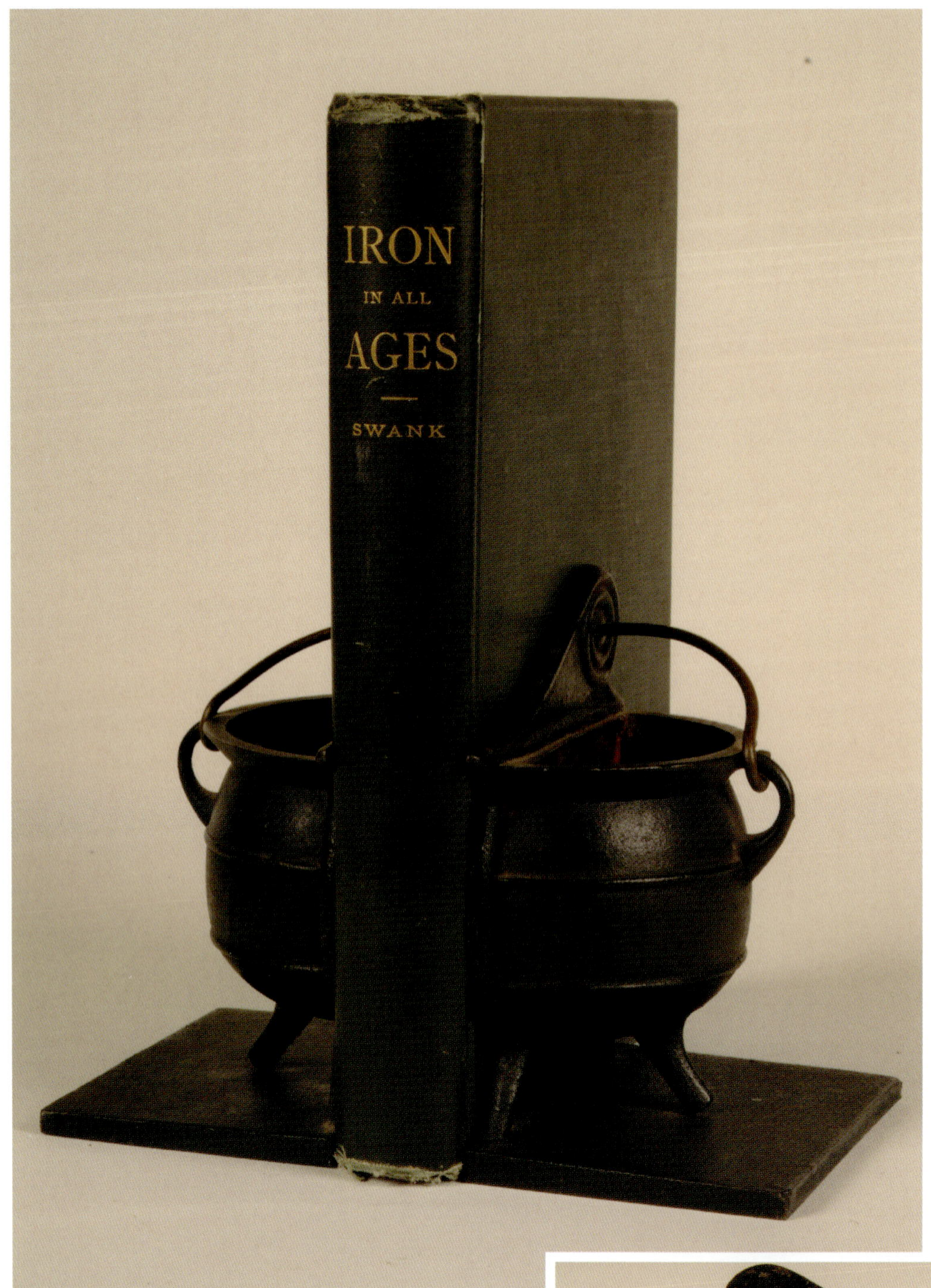

Pot bookends, cast iron, copper, American, ca. 1920–1950. Height 5.5", width 4.25". A small half pot with mold seam through oval section cow's horn ears.

Pot is riveted to a scrolled back with a paper label showing a blast furnace and reading "Old Carlisle Iron, Gale-Decker Co." A copper wire bail is attached.

Pot, cast iron, brass, American, ca. 1920–1950. Height 3.5", rim diameter 3.875". Two-part mold with seam vertically through cow's horn ears, gate on bottom ground off. Triangular-section legs cast first and laid in mold. Original brass wire bail. A miniature identical to the bookend pots.

Triangular-section tapered legs were cast first and laid into the mold before the body was cast.

Pot, cast iron, American, ca. 1920–1950. Height 4.5", rim diameter 5.75". Another probable Gale-Decker pot cast in a two-part mold with cow's horn ears and a gate on the bottom ground away. Bail is missing.

Two pots, cast iron, American. Left pot: ca. 1930–1960. Height 2.375", rim diameter 2.5", lid missing, gate on bottom ground off. Two-part mold parting through angular ears, early form. Right pot: ca. 1870–1900, height 2.875", rim diameter 2.5". A miniature of early slope-sided form cast in a two-part mold, gate on the bottom ground off. Angular ears and round-section peg legs.

Glue pot, cast iron, wrought iron, American, ca. 1850–1900. Height 5", diameter 7". Angular form cast in two-part mold parted horizontally at the widest diameter, gate on bottom. Vertical tab ears had wrought iron bail. Lacking tin or iron inner pot. Water heated in the outer vessel melted chunks of glue in the inner pot. Marked "2" on shoulder.

Pot cast iron, brass, American, ca. 1920–1950. Height 5.625", rim diameter 5". Heavy casting with two-part mold parting through the ears. This is not a cooking pot but a Cape Cod Fire Lighter.

These lighters, minus the lid and ceramic torch, are sometimes sold as cooking pots. With a brass lid and bail, they held kerosene to soak the ceramic torch, which was lit and used to start a fire.

Chapter 4

CAST IRON KETTLES

Some writers have treated pots and kettles as synonymous terms; they are not. *The Oxford English Dictionary*, quoting Samuel Johnson's Dictionary of 1755 sets forth the difference clearly: "In the kitchen the name of pot is given to the boiler that grows narrower towards the top, and of kettle to that which grows wider."[1] They are different vessels, hence their separate treatment here.

Pots presented more difficulty in the casting process since they had a core contained within a sphere. Patterns and "cheeks," or molding flasks, had to separate in two or more sections for the removal of the patterns prior to casting.

Kettles presented a simpler casting procedure. The kettle, with its outward-sloping straight or curved sides, needed no two part patterns as did a pot. Another kettle shorn of legs and ears would serve, and could be easily lifted away from its core in the preparation of the mold. Ears and legs were molded as they were for pots, and their changes in form were the same. Cast bottom up as were pots, kettles may bear gate marks and ghost gates from the kettle used as a pattern.

Vessels of kettle form have been cast in sand since the seventeenth century.[2] However, very large kettles for sugar mills, butchering, potash making, and the like were cast in a pit using loam-molding technology similar to that for casting bells. Clay was formed over a center of bricks in a pit for the core, shaped by a rotating wooden sweep. The clay was heated, dusted with charcoal, and the clay wall thickness molded, dried, and dusted. The outer layer or cope was applied and dried. The cope sat on a wide ring enabling it to be lifted off to remove the inner layer of loam. It was then replaced and the kettle could be cast.[3]

Large vessels of heavy weight might be cast lip up, a very specialized technique since the core had to hang suspended within the mold. This technique made a better kettle since it insured the bottom would have enough solid metal.[4]

Many kettles of New England origin have a distinctive ear that is an extension of the rim upwards on opposite sides sufficient to enclose a hole for the bail. This ear form further simplified the casting process since there were no ear patterns to install and remove.[5] (See page 81.)

Early kettle forms were straight-sided, widening to the rim or nearly vertical, and usually wider than they were tall. By 1800, a more rounded form with a fully curved bottom replaced the earlier type. These were made into the mid-nineteenth century, after which they reverted to a straight sided but taller form.

Kettles widen out from the bottom to the rim and are simpler to cast than pots. Kettle ears and legs are similar to those found on pots.

Kettle, cast iron, wrought iron, American, ca. 1730–1760. Height 6", rim diameter 9.5". Early deep-bellied New England form with ears as an upward extension of the rim. Original square-section wrought iron bail.

Gate on bottom. D section legs, one leg molded crooked.

Kettle, cast iron, wrought iron, American, ca. 1750. Height 8.5", rim diameter 13". New England form with ear tabs. Gate is short and thick, an early type. Heavy D section legs. Original square-section wrought iron bail.

Marked in four places around sides with an early Federal eagle over initials "J. P." Possibly cast by Joshua Porter, operator of Salisbury Furnace at Lakeville, Connecticut, during the Revolution, or by John Phelps, ironmaster at the Stafford, Connecticut, furnace in 1779.[6]

Kettle, cast iron, American, ca. 1780. Height 3.75", rim diameter 5". New England form with raised ears, one not pierced for a bail. Possibly a small camp kettle for individual use. Short D-section legs. Heavy gate.

LEFT to RIGHT:

Kettle, cast iron, wrought iron, American, ca. 1808. Height 6.5", rim diameter 9.5". New England form with heavy D section legs. Original square-section wrought iron bail.

Marked "1808" in two places on the bottom. Cast using a gate. This kettle is identical to one cast at the Salisbury, Connecticut, furnace.[7]

Kettle, cast iron, wrought iron, American, ca. 1800. Height 12", rim diameter 18". New England type of a more rounded post 1790 form.[8] A mold mark runs horizontally around the base, indicating casting in a two-part mold. D section fire-eroded legs. Original wrought iron square-section bail with decorative scrolled ends.

Bottom has two gates since this is a large vessel.

Kettle, cast iron, wrought iron, American, ca. 1820–1830. Height 5.375, rim diameter 7". New England rounded form with molded lappets below ears. A thin casting with an elongated gate and triangular-section legs. Wrought iron replaced bail. A crack extends down from the rim on the right side.

LEFT to RIGHT:

Kettle, cast iron, steel, American, ca. 1750–1780. Height 5.5", rim diameter 6.25". Mid-Atlantic states type with pot-style ears, angular and of triangular section. Steel replaced bail.

Large gate, round-section legs. Molten iron puddled at the gate was not fluid enough when it was cast.

Kettle, cast iron, steel, American, ca. 1770–1790. Height 6", rim diameter 8.5". Deep flat-bottom form. Round-section, slightly curved ears. Replaced steel bail. Short D-section legs, long, thin gate.

Original cast lid with ringed astragal moldings and handle, marked "1" as is the bottom of the kettle.

Kettle, cast iron, wrought iron, American, ca. 1770–1810. Height 5.625", rim diameter 6.5". Tapered triangular-section ears, triangular-section legs. Short, thick gate. Original wrought iron round-section bail.

Kettle, cast iron, wrought iron, Pennsylvania, ca. 1760–1780. Height 6.75", rim diameter 9.5". A baking kettle, it has no legs and a flat bottom. Angular ears of round-section, gate on bottom. Original square-section wrought iron bail. Used for baking brown bread, this type was sometimes called a "French" kettle.[9] They were often given a lid.

Kettle, cast iron, wrought iron, American, ca. 1810–1830. Height 6.625", rim diameter 8.625". Rounded nineteenth-century form with rounded ears. D section legs, thin gate. Original wrought iron bail. Original cast lid. Cast using a much cracked kettle as a pattern; the original's cracks are seen on this casting.

Kettle, cast iron, wrought iron, American, ca. 1780–1800. Height 9", rim diameter 10". Deep flat-bottomed form with a large gate. Triangular-section ears curved slightly on the inside, heavy triangular-section legs set well under with little splay. Original wrought iron bail with curls on loop ends. This may be a Pine Grove Furnace product.

Kettle, cast iron, wrought iron, American, ca. 1830–1850. Height 5.875", rim diameter 9.75". Deep inset bottom for stove top use indicates a post 1830 date. Curved triangular-section ears, peg legs. Gate on bottom. Original wrought iron bail.

LEFT to RIGHT:

Kettle, cast iron, steel, American, ca. Kettle, cast iron, wrought iron, American, ca. 1832–1845. Height 7", rim diameter 10.5". A shallow form with a section of the rim extended out and up for the ear. D-section legs, large gate. Original wrought iron bail.

Marked on side "ARCOLE IRONWORKS W.S. & CO". The Arcole Furnace, Geauqa County, Ohio, was begun by John Wilkeson in 1830 and used bog ore. The Arcole Co. was the largest industrial plant in Ohio in 1835.[10]

Kettle, cast iron, American, ca. 1840–1870. Height 7.5", rim diameter 10.5". A baking kettle derived from the earlier "French" kettle form. Deep inset pit bottom with three peg legs. Horizontal lifting tabs project from the rim. This kettle probably had a lid originally.[11]

Cast lid marked "L. H. ROGAN & CO. KNOXVILLE, TEN. No. 3". Cast using a sprue.

Kettle, cast iron, steel, American, ca. 1850–1870. Height 8.5", rim diameter 11.375". Later full-round form with round-section cow's horn ears typical of post 1850 castings. Small D section legs. Replaced steel bail. Small gate on bottom.

Kettle, cast iron, wrought iron, American, ca. 1890–1910. Height 8.25", rim diameter 10.5". Straight sides with gate at rim ground away. Horizontal tabs for original wire bail, peg legs, pouring ring on side.

Peg legs. Marked "WAGNER 8" on the bottom for Wagner Manufacturing Co., Sidney, Ohio.[12]

Kettle, cast iron, steel , French, ca. 1750. Height 4.5", rim diameter 5". A French form with round-section curved ears. The curved ear was used earlier in France than in America where it is usually (with some exceptions found at Saugus) later nineteenth century. Replaced steel bail. Gate on the bottom.

Legs are triangular in section with reeded fronts. The large pad feet are typically French.

Kettle, cast iron, wrought iron, French, ca. 1850. Height 6", rim diameter 7". A thin casting. Triangular-section legs with no feet have moldings on the front sides and are hollowed on the back. Gate on the bottom. Original wrought iron bail has a raised rectangular section to center it on a trammel hook. Most of these kettles originally had cast lids with small vent pipes.[13]

The French round-section, curved ear patterns have the top horizontal piece covering the end of the curved vertical section. American and English ears have a rabbet or butt joint to the vertical piece.

Brazier, cast iron, steel, wrought iron, American, ca. 1830–1850. Height 8.5", rim diameter 12". A straight-sided kettle form with triangular-section ears curved inside and out. Gate on the bottom. Steel grate and gridiron top replaced, originals would have been cast iron. Triangular-section legs, original wrought iron bail. This unusual vessel could be used in any situation where a portable stove was desired.

Large butchering kettle, cast iron, steel, wrought iron, beef, American, ca. 1880–1900. Height 27", rim diameter 27". A large flanged lip facilitates setting in a brickwork range. This vessel finds a new use as a charcoal grill. It sits in an antique wrought iron "three foot." Other large, unwieldy kettles have been found useful as wood or kindling holders by the fireplace. Many rust their remaining years in the landscape as flower planters.

Chapter 5

CAST IRON DUTCH OVENS

The Dutch oven is a wide, relatively shallow kettle form with a flat bottom and straight, slightly flared sides. It has two ears for a bail. The bail is usually not permanently attached to the ears and is often a two-part hinged type that adjusts to the width of the vessel. The bail is also used as a double hook to raise the lid. The cast lid has a center arched handle and a raised outer lip. It fits snugly into a recess in the oven rim. In use the oven sits over coals on the hearth. Coals are also placed on the lid where they are retained by the raised rim. Baking is thus accomplished between the two fires.

The Dutch oven may have evolved from the skillet form, some of which were sold with lids.1 Seventeenth and eighteenth-century low, wide skillets sometimes have ledged rims to fit a lid, but these may not all have had raised rims for the coals.[2] (See page 127.)

The Dutch oven as we know it appears to have come into widespread use in the second half of the eighteenth century.[3] By the 1770s and 1780s, many furnaces were casting them in large numbers. Pine Grove Furnace in Cumberland County, Pennsylvania, cast 1743 ovens in small, medium, and large sizes in 1786, second only in number to the 3351 pots cast.[4] By the early nineteenth century, the "bake oven" was an essential element of the pioneer kitchen where a built in brick oven might be lacking.[5]

Dating of Dutch ovens is primarily through the progression of the ear changes, as with pots and kettles. Handled examples sometimes called "hearth ovens"[6] are a variant of the spider form having a lid with a raised rim to hold coals. They may have been called spiders during the nineteenth century.[7] Later (1850–1920) examples are often marked by the maker on the lid. By 1900, legs had begun to shrink. Modern examples have legs half or one third as long as earlier types. Earlier legs were triangular in section and tapered. Later (1880–1900) legs were round in section.

By the mid-nineteenth century, as stoves replaced the open hearth, Dutch ovens came to be used more in camping or chuck-wagon situations. A form with no legs and a fitted lid without the high rim to hold coals was produced beginning around 1840 for stove top use. Some makers called this a Dutch oven; by others it was called a French baking pan.8 A variant of the Dutch oven was the fish kettle. This was an oval or elongated, deep version of the Dutch oven having four legs. They were sold with and without lids.[9] (See page 96, bottom.)

Although made in large numbers during the nineteenth century, Dutch ovens are fairly rare today, especially with original lids, many of which were dropped on the hearth and broken. The straight sides and sharp angle to the flat base also made a form that cracked easily, so many did not survive heavy use.

The Dutch oven is a shallow, kettle-like form with a lid, having a raised flange to hold hot coals. It served as a baking vessel in pioneer homes lacking a built-in brick oven.

Dutch Oven, cast iron, wrought iron, American, ca. 1800–1820. Height 6.25", rim diameter 13". D-section ears curved inside and out. Triangular-section legs. Short, thick gate.

Hinged, adjustable bail is detached to enable lifting of lid as well as an oven.

Lid with gate on underside, raised lip to contain hot coals, 13.25" diameter.

Dutch Oven, cast iron, wrought iron, American, ca. 1820–1840. Height 6.5", rim diameter 10.25". A deep (4.25") oven, gate on the bottom. Triangular-section ears with a curve out and upward typical of the 1840s. Light triangular-section legs. Original wrought iron attached bail.

Marked on lid "BLACKLOCK FOUNDRY SOUTH PITTSBURG TENN." The Blacklock Foundry was begun in 1896 and became the Lodge Co. in 1910. It is still in business.[10]

Hearth Oven, cast iron, American, ca. 1896–1910. Height 4", rim diameter 10". The hearth oven has a lid to hold coals and an attached handle. It is smaller than the Dutch oven but used in the same way. Round-section legs are typical for ca. 1900, as is the teardrop hole in the handle.

Dutch Oven, cast iron, wrought iron, American, ca. 1840–1860. Height 4", rim diameter 7.875". Oven form with straight sides and flat bottom for use on a stove. Gate on the bottom. Lid has a handle and is marked "8". Original wrought iron wire bail.

Round-section ears curve out and up, typical for 1840–1860. This recurving ear is also found on pots of this period.

TOP to BOTTOM:

Fish Kettle, cast iron, American, ca. 1790–1810. Height 9.5", length 22", width 12". This rare variant of the Dutch oven was called an oval oven or fish kettle.[11] They were sold with or without lids. Heavy triangular-section legs. Thick gate.

Triangular-section ears curved inside and out.

Chapter 6

CAST IRON TEAKETTLES

Various sizes of water boilers for general household use are generally called teakettles. Typically water boiled in a teakettle would be poured over loose tea in a smaller, ceramic tea pot. Teakettles were not used to brew tea. Since it is a widely accepted term, teakettles will be used here when describing water boilers.

Cast iron teakettles were first produced in America about 1760–1765 in Carver, Massachusetts.[1] These eighteenth century teakettles were shaped like a squashed onion with a gooseneck spout, a form that lasted into the first decade of the nineteenth century. (See page 99.) The Charlotte Furnace in South Carver, built by Bartlett Murdock in 1760 and operated later as a foundry by the Ellis family, cast teakettles, but others soon produced them as well.[2] Teakettles marked "M Ellis & Co 1866" may be commemorative pieces marking the one hundredth anniversary of teakettle production by this company.

Because they were difficult to mold, teakettles were not produced by early furnaces in large numbers, as were pots and kettles. In 1786, Pine Grove Furnace in Cumberland County, Pennsylvania, cast 3351 pots, 335 kettles, and 1743 Dutch ovens, but only 109 teakettles. Jeremiah Lammerson was the only molder of the several men employed with the expertise needed to mold teakettles.[3]

Teakettle patterns were valuable and may sometimes have been owned by others. A list of patterns available at the Carlisle Iron Works in Boiling Springs, Pennsylvania, in 1765 mentions that "A teakettle pattern can be had from Carlisle" obviously a specialty not included among those held at the ironworks.[4]

Like pots, patterns for teakettle bodies were composed of two halves. The molds were also of three parts. The spout, the most difficult part to mold correctly, was composed of four pattern sections. Pre 1846 teakettles will show mold marks running from rim to midsection on opposite sides similar to pots. A horizontal line runs around the circumference and through the base of the spout, which has a mark dividing it in half. The upper spout is also of two parts divided vertically. (See page 101.)

Early eighteenth century spouts had smaller passages than later ones. As time went on, spouts became larger to prevent clogging from calcium deposits. As spouts evolved into more practical, larger types, they also became less attractive.

In 1846 Ezra Ripley was granted a patent whereby teakettles could be cast in a two-part mold that parted horizontally. The parting line divided the spout into top and bottom sections along with the body. The spout was an integral part of top and bottom pattern halves, thus obviating the need for separate spout molding.[5] From this time on, spouts became wider and shorter until by 1900 they were mere vestigial troughs.

Teakettles (water boilers) show a progression over time from classical forms to designs predicated on optimum efficiency in casting as well as use on the stove rather than over an open fire. Changes in form, bail design, and lids are important dating indicators.

Teakettle chart.

uninspired if not downright ugly and spouts had become minimal. (See page 121.)

As the cookstove replaced the open fire in the 1830–1850 period, more teakettles were made with inset or "pit" bottoms to fit within a circular stove lid hole. Legs were always short but became mere stubs only long enough to keep the teakettle stable on the flat stove top. Early teakettles were always made to hang over a fire, never with long legs to stand over coals as pots were.

Lids were loose on older teakettles and many are now missing due to falling on the hearth and breaking. Lids on older teakettles are often not original. Early lids have the gate or sprue mark on the outer top rather than the inner surface. They tend to have a low-domed form with molded ridges and cast-in wire ring handles. (See page 100, bottom left.) By 1820, lids were lighter with flattened domes, gates moved to the inner side, and ring handles gave way to a flat vertical finger grip. (See page 101.)

Teakettle forms evolved as well from pleasing classical forms to dumpy shapes determined more by ease of manufacture than eye appeal. The onion form became more full or rounded by 1790–1810. (See page 102, top.) By 1840, teakettles tended to be more angular, sloping down to a sharp shoulder from the rim and then angled in to the base. (See page 105.) Ripley's patent facilitated the adoption of this form. More rounded shapes returned in the 1850–1880 period with wider spouts. (See page 117.) All of these later shapes were cast in two-part molds with parting lines around the body and running out of the spout. By 1900, shapes were

By the 1840–1850 era, some lids were hinged so as to lift up. By the 1860s, the lid that swings to the side was devised and remained standard through 1900. (See page 116.)

Handles or bails in eighteenth century teakettles were made of flat wrought iron hammered into small round hooks at each end by blacksmiths who worked at the furnace where they were cast. By the 1820s, many of these were being made of round stock. A special type of concave, narrow band hammered at the ends into a small round section hook to pivot in the ear tabs appeared around 1859 and became universal until a wire handle with a wooden or spiral spring grip replaced it after 1880. (See page 114.)

The weight of teakettles decreased from 1760 to 1900, as with pots and kettles, with particularly thin and light examples being cast in the 1840–1880 period.

TOP to BOTTOM:

Long, thin gate typical of teakettles, short legs only long enough to prevent tipping.

Teakettle, cast iron, wrought iron, American, ca. 1760–1780. Height 7.5", diameter 9". Early flat-bottom onion form with gooseneck spout. Three-part mold, spout pattern in four parts. Original lid with wire loop handle broken off, gate on top. Handle with crimped ends to prevent swiveling is old but not original.

Marked on back in oval cartouche "JOHN MAXIM".

LEFT to RIGHT:

Teakettle, cast iron, wrought iron, American, ca. 1770–1780. Height 6.5", diameter 8.5". Early onion form with gooseneck spout. Original wrought iron bail, lid ca. 1820–1830 is not original. Three-part mold with long, thin gate and short legs.

Marked on back in oval cartouche "T : A", possibly for Peter Townsend and William Alexander, operator and owner respectively of Sterling Furnace, Orange County, New York.[6]

Teakettle, cast iron, wrought iron, American, ca. 1770–1800. Height 7.875", diameter 9". Onion form cast in three-part mold with a gooseneck spout. Original lid is attached to a heavy wrought iron bail with a chain to prevent its dropping onto the hearth and breaking.

Round section gooseneck spout.

Teakettle, cast iron, wrought iron, American, ca. 1780–1820. Height 8", diameter 8.75". Onion form with higher sides and more rounded bottom. Three-part mold, short legs, original wrought iron bail. Original lid with finger grip, gate on the inside typical of ca. 1810–1830.

Oversize gooseneck spout. By the early nineteenth century spouts were becoming larger in an attempt to prevent clogging with calcium deposits.

TOP to BOTTOM:

Teakettle, cast iron, wrought iron, American, ca. 1780–1810. Height 7", diameter 9.5". High rounded form, three-part mold, gooseneck spout. Original wrought iron, wide bail. Lid replaced with a sheet-iron replica. Short legs.

This heavily rusted kettle was dug up from the ruins of the Green Tree tavern in Cumberland County, Pennsylvania, burned in 1833.[7] It is an exact copy of the preceding example, here photographed with it. It may be a product of Pine Grove Furnace since others of the same design have been found in the area.

Teakettle, cast iron, wrought iron, American, ca. 1770–1810. Height 10.5", diameter 9.75". High form used for larger vessels with tilting lever enabling pouring while hanging from a trammel hook. Three-part mold, original wrought iron bail, original lid, short legs, gooseneck spout.

Marked "J K" in oval cartouche on back. Possibly cast at John King's furnace in Taunton, Massachusetts, an early, prolific maker of teakettles according to Swank's *History of Iron in all Ages*.

Teakettle, cast iron, wrought iron, American, ca. 1800–1830. Height 11", diameter 10". A tilting kettle, later than the preceding one and of lighter weight. Three-part mold, long gate, D section short legs. Lid with early style ring handle and gate on outside may not be original. Original round-section wrought iron bail.

LEFT to RIGHT:

Teakettle, cast iron, wrought iron, American, ca. 1790–1810. Height 7.5", diameter 9.25". Fully-rounded form with a large gooseneck spout. Three-part mold with gate, one inch long legs, original wrought iron bail.

The large spout curves back slightly, then up and forward creating a most attractive teakettle spout.

Teakettle, cast iron, wrought iron, American, ca. 1800–1820. Height 9", diameter 9". Straight sides with high, rounded shoulder, three-part mold with gate. Peg feet, gooseneck spout. Original wrought iron bail. Stepped lid typical of ca. 1820 with short gate on inside.

Teakettle, cast iron, wrought iron, American, ca. 1820–1830. Height 7", diameter 8.25". Angular, straight-sided form, three-part mold with long, thin gate, no feet. Original round-section wrought iron bail. Stepped lid.

Teakettle, cast iron, wrought iron, American, ca. 1830. Height 8", diameter 9". High-shoulder form with slightly curved sides, three-part mold with long, thin gate. Pronounced ovoid shape to spout base. Button feet, original wrought iron bail. Stepped lid with gate on inside, replaced knob handle.

Gooseneck spout is now becoming oval where it joins the body.

Teakettle, cast iron, wrought iron, American, ca. 1830–1840. Height 5.75", diameter 8.5". Angular sharp-shouldered form, three-part mold, long thin gate. Oval base to spout. Peg feet, original wrought iron bail. Stepped lid with knob handle.

Teakettle, cast iron, wrought iron, American, ca. 1835–1845. Height 10.5", diameter 9.5". Angular-shouldered form with early, deep inset pit bottom for stove top use. Three-part mold with thin gate, ovoid-base gooseneck spout. Early use of concave, narrow strip, hammered into hooks at the ends for bail.

Fluted lid has tab finger grip.

Lid interior is back-coped (pattern is hollowed on back to save metal), a practice prevalent in castings after this time. Sprue on interior.

Teakettle, cast iron, wrought iron, American, ca. 1840–1850. Height 9", diameter 10.5". Angular form with more shallow pit bottom than earlier vessels. Three-part mold with long, thin gate. Peg feet, oval base to spout. Round stock wrought iron bail, replaced tin lid. A thin casting, as is typical in this period.

Teakettle, cast iron, wrought iron, American, ca. 1850. A heavy vessel cast in a two-part mold with the horizontal-parting line extending through the bottom of the spout, which is of the older round-section type. A new form angling out from the base to a vertical-ribbed side, then sloped into lid. Bail is wrought iron round stock.

Stepped lid with a long finger grip. This vessel came from Utica, New York, where there were several stove foundries that likely made holloware as well. It is an early use of the two-part mold.

Teakettle, cast iron, wrought iron, American, ca. 1838–1845. Height 8", diameter 7.5". High-shouldered form cast in a two-part mold. Wrought iron bail of narrow concave stock hammered down at the ends into hooks. Stepped lid with a brass knob.

Marked on shoulder in oval cartouche "J. SAVERY & SON NEW YORK". Made at the foundry in Jersey City of John Savery, born in 1789 in Carver, Massachusetts, in business under this name 1838–1845.[8]

Marked on opposite shoulder in an oval cartouche "PHOENIX WORKS No. 4"

Horizontal-parting line extends up top of spout, which is of round section with a low-arched top section. The two-part mold that encompassed the spout as an integral mold part was the invention of Ezra Ripley in 1846.[9] This example may have preceded his patent as the business name changed to John Savery & Sons in January of 1846.[10]

Thin gate across bottom. Note three decorative star-shaped button feet. This vessel has many decorative details.

Teakettle, cast iron, wrought iron, American, ca. 1840–1855. Height 7.375", diameter 9". Three-angled body cast in a two-part mold, gate on the bottom. Lid with original brass knob marked "M & B PATENT". Wrought iron bail of flattened-oval stock.

Bottom showing a long, thin gate and a rim around the base, which serves as a pit bottom for a stove hole.

Two-part mold includes bottom and top of spout. Front of spout molded using a third pattern. This is an intermediate step between early spouts molded using four patterns and Ripley's patent wherein the spout is an integral part of each half of the teakettle pattern.

Teakettle, cast iron, wrought iron, American, ca. 1840–1855. Height 5.75", diameter 8". Similar to the previous vessel with the same mold and spout features. Lid with gate on interior and original brass knob, marked "M & S PATENT". Original wrought iron half-round section bail.

Lift-off lids from the two previous teakettles.

Teakettle, cast iron, wrought iron, American, ca. 1850. Height 5", diameter 5.25". Angled body cast in a two-part mold, gate on the bottom, tab feet. Gooseneck spout with the bottom a part of the body pattern and the top using two vertical half patterns. Old wire bail.

Teakettle, cast iron, wrought iron, American, ca. 1850–1870. Height 9", diameter 8". Rounded form. Two-part pattern and mold includes spout. Pit bottom marked "6" with a long, thin gate. Original wrought iron round-section bail.

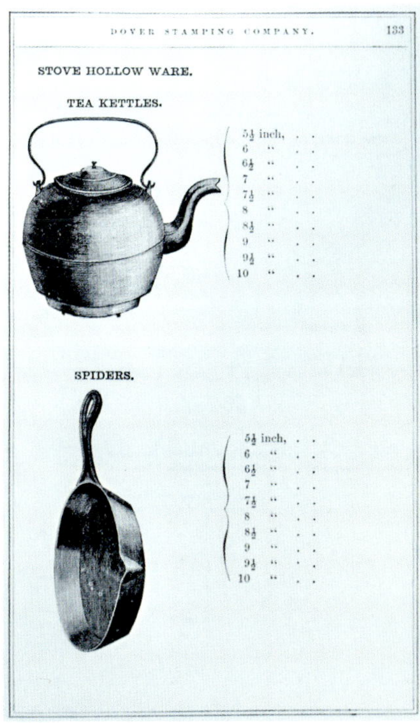

DOVER STAMPING COMPANY. 133

STOVE HOLLOW WARE.

TEA KETTLES.

5½ inch, . .
6 " . .
6½ " . .
7 " . .
7½ " . .
8 " . .
8½ " . .
9 " . .
9½ " . .
10 " . .

SPIDERS.

5½ inch, . .
6 " . .
6½ " . .
7 " . .
7½ " . .
8 " . .
8½ " . .
9 " . .
9½ " . .
10 " . .

An exact cut of this vessel is in the Dover Stamping Co. catalog for 1869.[11]

Teakettle, cast iron, wrought iron, American, ca. 1850. Height 9", diameter 6.75". Rounded form with inset pit bottom. Two-part mold, ovoid gooseneck spout. Lid with knob atop octagonal facets, sprue on inside. Wrought iron bail of narrow concave stock hammered down at ends used extensively until 1880–1900.

Gate and three button feet on base. Marked "A & L 5", for Abbot & Lawrence of Philadelphia, Pennsylvania.[12]

The hinged swing-up lid was a feature of some teakettles until 1860–1870 when lids swinging to the side became common.

Teakettle, cast iron, wrought iron, American, ca. 1850–1860. Height 7.5", diameter 8.5". Angular body cast in two-part mold. Gooseneck spout with rounded bottom and three-sided top typical of 1850–1870. Marked "5" on shoulder. Wrought iron bail of concave stock, short gate on flat bottom.

Teakettle, cast iron, wrought iron, American, ca. 1850–1860. Height 6.5", diameter 7.75". Marked "MARIETTA" on top of the hinged swing-up lid. Two part pattern and mold with parting line running up spout. Thin gate on the bottom. Wrought iron bail of flattened oval section forged down at the ends into hooks.

This vessel is somewhat crudely cast and heavy for its size. Brazed repairs to the pattern are visible in the cast finished product near the "4" mark. In addition, there is a repair to the teakettle rear-bail ear where a new hole was drilled after the top of the ear broke off.

Teakettle, cast iron, wrought iron, American, ca. 1860s. Height 6", diameter 10.5". Angular body similar to 1840s style with short, wide, trough spout at top of shoulder. Two-part mold with long gate and three stub feet. Wrought iron bail of narrow, flattened oval stock.

Marked on swing-away (to side) lid "Mc FARLAND & TURNER IND. PA". The swing-away lid and trough spout, of which this is an early example, became common by the 1880s.

Teakettle, cast iron, wrought iron, American, ca. 1859–1867. Height 9", diameter 11". A large teakettle of a rounded form. Two-part mold with pit bottom and gate. Wrought iron bail of concave stock.

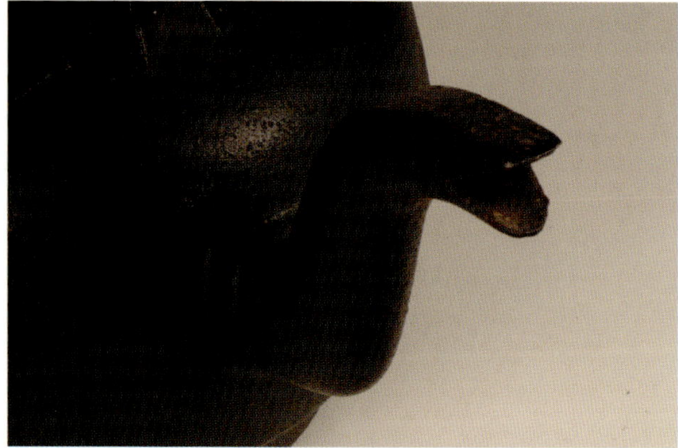

Gooseneck spout with rounded lower section and three-sided top. The parting line for the body runs out the spout, dividing it into top and bottom sections.

Swing-up lid marked "LEIBRANDT & M'DOWELL PHILA". Body marked "10" on shoulder. This firm went into business in 1859.[13] By 1867 they were using a similar, patented lid.

Teakettles, cast iron, wrought iron, American, ca. 1870s. Left height 7.875", diameter 9.25", right height 6.25", diameter 7.25". Both of round-shoulder form, two-part molds parting horizontally through the spouts. Gates on slightly concave bases eliminating the need for button feet. Wrought iron bails. Left of flattened round stock, right of narrow concave stock, both forged down at the ends.

The kettle on the right has the older more pronounced gooseneck spout with rounded bottom, now more full where it joins the body and having a three-sided top. The kettle on the left has the rounded, full-bellied, short gooseneck spout that becomes standard on most teakettles from the 1860s to 1880s.

The swing-up lids of both teakettles are similarly marked. They were cast as a semi-circular unit with a mounting base riveted to the body. The lid from the smaller teakettle is marked "LEIBRANDT & M'DOWELL PHILAD'A 5".

Patent date of 1867 on underside of lid.

Teakettle, cast iron, wrought iron, American, ca. 1866. Height 9.375", diameter 10.5". Rounded body with pit bottom. Two-part mold with older style gooseneck spout. Peg feet, long-thin gate. Original wrought iron bail.

Swing-away lid with original brass knob marked "M ELLIS & CO. SO. CARVER MASS. 1866". Matt Ellis & Co. traced its roots to the Charlotte Furnace of Carver, Massachusetts, built in 1756. Here the first cast iron teakettles made in America were produced in the 1760s.[14] This teakettle may commemorate that event.

Teakettle, cast iron, wrought iron, American, ca. 1860–1880. Height 8", diameter 9". Rounded form cast in a two-part mold with a long gate. Bellied-gooseneck spout, original wrought iron bail. Swing-up lid marked "SPRINGVILLE STOVE & HOLLOW WARE WORKS PA". Bottom marked "6 QTS". Springville is in Chester County, Pennsylvania.

LEFT to RIGHT:

Teakettle, cast iron, wrought iron, wood, American, ca. 1861–1879. Height 8", diameter 10". Rounded form with pit bottom and long gate. Two-part mold with bellied spout. Original iron-wire bail with wooden grip. The wire bail obviated the need to forge down concave stock into hooks at each end since it could be bent cold.

Swing-away lid marked "JOHN A. GOEWAY ALBANY N.Y." Goeway was in business from 1861 to 1879.[15]

LEFT to RIGHT:

Teakettle, cast iron, wrought iron, American, ca. 1860–1880. Height 6.25", diameter 8". Form angles out from base then curves in at shoulder, long thin gate. Two-part mold with bellied spout. Original wrought iron, flattened, round-section bail.

Swing-away lid marked "POCASSET IRON WORKS NEW YORK", marked "4" on bottom.

Teakettle, cast iron, wrought iron, American(?), ca. 1870–1890. Height 7", length 11". Ovoid straight-sided body with flange acting as a pit bottom. Two-part mold with a gate. Bellied spout. Original wrought iron concave-section bail with forged ends.

Swing-away lid marked "Co-Operative Foundry Co. JEWEL" with eagle over crown. This vessel was made to fit a specific stove.

LEFT to RIGHT:

Teakettle, cast iron, wrought iron, American, ca. 1871–1874. Height 5", width of body 7". Rectangular body cast in a two-part mold with a gate. Bellied spout. Original wrought iron bail of flattened-round stock. Angled side flange fits into the side of a special stove, the "Winter proof Base Burner" made by A. Ingraham & Co. of Troy, New York, which was in business from 1871 to 1874.[16]

The rectangular lid has an angled flange with mouse-like ears. It is marked "S Spoors Pat. 1869 A. 12-13", the body is marked on top "TROY. N.Y." Traces of an original coat of white enamel remain on this vessel. S. Spoor of Phelps, New York, patented a "boiling kettle" on February 23, 1869.[17] The rectangular design is prone to cracking and is clumsy to pour because the handle is not balanced.

Teakettle, cast iron, wrought iron, American, ca. 1870s. Height 5", body 7.25" wide. Rectangular body cast in a two-part mold with a gate, bellied spout with faceted top. Zinc-plated exterior. Original wrought iron concave-section bail attached at tip of the spout and front of the body.

Lid with a decorative flange is marked "S. Spoors PATTENT[*sic*] H. L. 12". Body is marked "TROY. N. Y." and spout top is marked "S 7. 13". The lid is repaired.

LEFT to RIGHT:

Two teakettles, cast iron, American, ca. 1860–1880. Both heights 9", diameters 9.5" Rounded form with pit bottom. Two-part mold with parting line sweeping from the widest diameter up to the top of a stubby spout. These kettles were made by two different foundries from patterns purchased from a third party. The teakettle on the left has a cast handle, a lift-off lid, and a repair plug. The teakettle on the right has a wrought iron handle and a swing-away lid.

Swing-away lid marked "Lewisburg". A hole in the lid may be a casting flaw. The iron foundry in Lewisburg, Pennsylvania, operated from 1834–1875.

Teakettle, cast iron, wrought iron, American, ca. 1866. Height 8.5", diameter 9.5". Rounded body cast in a two-part mold with an angled-in pit bottom that is slightly-concave to clear a thin gate, marked "8" on top of the spout. Low stub feet worn flat. Original wrought iron bail with ends forged into hooks.

Swing-away lid marked "A. BRADLEY & CO. PITTSBURGH, PA. 1866".

Teakettle, cast iron, wrought iron, American, ca. 1860–1880. Height 8", diameter 10". Rounded body cast in a two-part mold with a stubby spout. Original wrought iron bail of curved section with forged ends.

Concave base of pit bottom allows the base to sit clear of the gate.

Domed swing-away lid marked "W. RESOR & CO. CINCINATTI PATENT APPLIED FOR".

LEFT to RIGHT:

Teakettle, cast iron, wrought iron, American, ca. 1880. Height 9", diameter 9.75". Rounded body cast in a two-part mold with a deep-bellied spout, zinc plated. Bottom with thin gate is marked "O.P & Co 8". Original wrought iron bail with forged ends.

Swing-away lid marked "ORR, PAINTER & CO READING, PA".

Teakettle, cast iron, wrought iron, American, ca. 1880–1920. Height 6.5", diameter 9.75". Rounded body cast in a two-part mold with a deep-bellied spout. Crude white enameled exterior. Pit bottom with long gate. Original wire bail is missing its wooden or spiral-wire grip.

Swing-away lid marked "WROUGHT IRON RANGE CO. ST. LOUIS MO."

Teakettle, cast iron, wrought iron, American, ca. 1890–1910. Height 8", diameter 9.5". Rounded body with a stubby spout cast in a two-part mold. Bottom marked "ERIE" has a gate. Original wire bail with a spiral-wire grip.

Swing-away lid marked "ERIE". This vessel was a product of the Griswold Manufacturing Co. of Erie, Pennsylvania.[18]

Teakettle, cast iron, tin, English, ca. 1932, Height to the top of the handle 9.375", diameter 7". Cast in a two-part mold parting vertically through the spout, gate at the top of side, rear ground away. Cast iron handle. This form was popular in England from the 1850s on. Marked "HOLCROFT 5 Pts..." with patent date of 1932 on the side, "AGA Made in England ESSE" on the opposite side. Brass plaque on top of the tin lid, handle stamped "T HOLCROFT & SONS . WOLVERHAMPTON".

Decorative diamond-shaped pad where handle is riveted to the body of the teakettle. Ground off seam.

Teakettle, cast iron, wrought iron, Scotland. ca. 1860–1900. Height to the handle top 7.25", diameter 6". A common late nineteenth century British form with a classic gooseneck spout.[19] Cast in a two-part mold.

The forged wrought iron handle with triangular pad ends riveted to the body is typically British, though some handles were made to pivot in the American fashion. High domed lift-off lid.

Marked on the bottom "FALLKIRK N^{O}. 2". The Fallkirk Iron Co. was established at Fallkirk near Glasgow, Scotland, in 1819 and was still operating in 1900.

Chapter 7

CAST IRON SKILLETS, SPIDERS, AND FRYING PANS

This section covers vessels that in modern times would be called sauce pans and frying pans. The old terms are confusing and often used differently in specific geographic areas or times.

For this study, a "posnet" is a small, three-legged pot of cauldron form with a handle extending to the side. It must have a bulbous form with the typical flaring rim. Posnets are generally a pre-seventeenth century form and are not known to have been made of cast iron in America; hence they are not illustrated here.[1]

A skillet is a straight-sided vessel on three legs with a handle extending to one side. It may be proportioned like the modern sauce pot or of a wider, more shallow form.[2] Bottoms may be rounded and there is usually a slight flare from bottom to rim. Rims may be lipped or inset to fit a lid. These occur in copper alloy and iron and are frequently miscalled posnets in the antique trade. During the years of their production, they were called skillets. Skillets retained a separate identity over the seventeenth and eighteenth centuries, but by the late nineteenth century had become synonymous with frying pans and spiders.

Skillet, spider, and fry pan are all names that have been applied to vessels with straight sides, usually wider than deep, sometimes having legs and flat or rounded bottoms. Although the nomenclature is confusing, their use for frying and boiling is clear.

The dictionary describes a spider as a pan on legs with a long handle for use over coals.[3] The term "spider" does not appear to pre-date 1800. It is not found in early household inventories or lists of products of iron furnaces. However, a list of wares made at the Laurel Furnace, built in 1797 on Laurel Run, Fayette County, Pennsylvania,[4] lists "flat and round bottom spiders and lids" in 1804.[5] The "Ware Book" of Pine Grove Furnace, Cumberland County, Pennsylvania, in 1814 lists spiders, skillets with and without lids, and frying pans, thus showing each having a separate identity at that time.[6] An inventory of 1831 for James Allaire's Howell Works in New Jersey lists spider and skillet patterns.[7] By 1859, *The Dictionary of Americanisms* of John Russell Bartlett said a spider was, "A cast iron frying pan with three legs."[8] By 1860, the spider had begun to morph into the frying pan. "Spider" denoted a pan with legs until the later nineteenth century, when the term became synonymous with skillet and fry-pan, the legs having shrunk to stubs for stove top use and then vanishing completely by 1900. The Dover Stamping Company Catalog of 1869 listed various sizes of frying pans without legs labeled as spiders.[9] By 1890 the Griswold Company of Erie, Pennsylvania, was marketing a frying pan with no legs with the logo of a spider with frying pan body on the bottom.[10] An indication of the combined terms spider and skillet is found in a price list of holloware made at Mary Ann Furnace, Berks

> Skillet, spider, and fry pan are all names that have been applied to vessels with straight sides, usually wider than deep, sometimes having legs and flat or rounded bottoms. Although the nomenclature is confusing, their use for frying and boiling is clear.

County, Pennsylvania, in 1850: "Spider skillets $0.56"[11] The term "spider" was peculiar to the United States.[12] A wrought iron variety with a deep rounded bottom was popular in early nineteenth century Pennsylvania.[13]

The flat-bottom, wide frying pan with low side walls dates at least to the sixteenth century in England where it is found enumerated in house inventories.[14] These were beaten wrought iron made by a blacksmith. Frying pans are listed in a 1622 list of articles necessary to settlers in Virginia.[15] The flat-bottomed frying pan could be set on a trivet over coals or made with an arched handle to hang from a trammel hook. Some frying pans had long legs. Cast iron frying pans with legs came into use in the eighteenth century.

Seventeenth and early eighteenth century cast skillets may have faceted legs and defined feet. Most throughout the eighteenth century had a tapering D-section leg, the flat surface to the inside. Legs were usually more triangular in section by the early nineteenth century and as with pots and kettles, they became lighter and more slender.

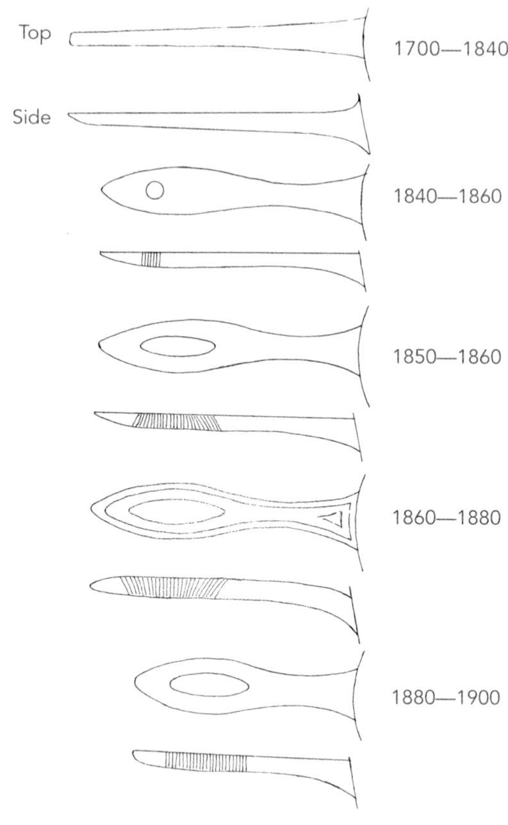

Skillet, spider, and fry pan handles remained a long, narrow type during the eighteenth century. They usually joined the side of the vessel partway down. The thin, teardrop form of the 1840s was usually flush with the rim. Later types remained in this position. By the later nineteenth century they had a slight upward bend.

Handles underwent changes as well. Seventeenth, eighteenth, and early nineteenth century handles were narrow, flat on the top, and rounded on the underside. They tapered slightly to the end where the termination was a slight undercut. Some had longitudinal flutes or ridges on the top or faceted undersides. In about 1840 these were replaced by a shorter, thin, flat handle of rounded teardrop shape with a narrowing waist close to the rim. Some have a round hole for hanging. By 1850-1860 the handle was given an elongated hole. In the 1860-1880 period the handles frequently had decorative mouldings around the hole. From about 1860 handles had an upward curve from the rim. The pointed ends of the 1840s became rounded and the holes rounded at the outer end by 1880-1890.

During the 1860-1890 period, castings became thin and smoothly finished, sometimes by lathe-turning the interior. By 1900, castings were becoming heavier, but still had smooth interiors. Pre-nineteen hundred frying pans had a raised circular ridge around the bottom so that the pan, with its slightly raised gate, would sit flat on a stove top. Early cast pans (1830-1840) may have stub feet to allow room for the gate. By 1920 most pans were flat-bottomed with casting gates on the rim ground off.

Griddles are not holloware since they are castings that need no core mold, but they are an important component of the cook's battery of utensils. Early examples are heavy and somewhat crude. Those intended for use "down hearth," standing directly on the hearth over coals, had legs about three inches long and handles projecting from the rear. Handles were usually minimally decorated. Legs were of the same types found on pots and kettles.

A refinement was the hanging griddle, allowing down hearth use or hanging over the fire from a crane or trammel hook. Some hung from a fixed, non-swiveling bail, others by a single curved arm, but most had swivels to allow rotation over the fire. Light griddles with wire bails that pivot side to side are later

(1860–1900) with bales intended for storage hanging, not for suspension over a fire.

Hanging griddles with legs are rare. A griddle cast with legs not equidistant would be unsteady since, like pots, they used three legs. By removing erroneously positioned legs when still hot from the casting, the piece could still be sold for use on a stove top or trivet. Furnaces sold griddles, sometimes called bake plates with or without legs.[16] By 1830–1850 most were cast without legs for use on stoves. Many griddles retained the eighteenth century rectangular handle, but were gated from the side to produce a flat bottom with no raised areas resulting from a gate on the bottom. A flat griddle bottom insured close contact with the stove top. By 1900 stove griddles were light castings with short handles akin to those on frypans.[17]

Skillet, cast iron, American, ca. 1644–1680. Height 6", diameter 9.5", handle 5". Probably cast at Braintree or Saugus, or at Winthrop's New Haven, Connecticut, furnace where many Saugus workers moved by 1660. A loam-molded vessel with pentagonal section legs widened at the foot in the style typical of Saugus.[18] Skillets were among the enumerated products of the short-lived Braintree furnace, and fragments have also been found at Saugus.[19]

Handle formed by a sprue broken from a previously cast vessel, inserted into the clay mold, and cast in. Everted rim for a lid. Late nineteenth century painted decoration may have helped to preserve this piece.

Sprue is centered on the bottom.

Small skillet, cast iron, American ca. 1644–1680, height 4.5", diameter 7.875". Loam molded. A crack going down from the rim, sprue handle with the end hammered to remove sharp edges of the end.

Skillet, cast iron, America, ca. 1723–1750. Height 4.5", diameter 9", handle 8". A heavy, almost flat-bottomed casting produced in a sand mold. Found in Fredericksburg, Virginia, this vessel may have originated at one of the furnaces operating in that area early in the eighteenth century: Tubal started in 1723, Accokeek in 1727, Fredericksville in 1729, or Spotswood's Massaponax foundry in 1730.[20]

The handle has a flat top and five faceted surfaces around the bottom. Faceted surfaces, whether on legs or on handles of holloware, are generally an early feature.

Large sprue on the bottom. The front legs are octagonal in section while the rear leg under the handle is of round section.

Skillet, cast iron, American, ca 1750. Height 6", diameter 8", handle 6.5". Deep form with everted rim, gate on the bottom. Widely splayed D-section legs. Typical narrow, tapered handle that is flat on top with a rounded underside.

Skillet, cast iron, American, ca. 1780–1800. Height 5.875", diameter 9.25", handle 8.75". Slightly rounded form with D-section legs widely splayed. Long-wide gate. Tapered handle.

Skillet, cast iron, American, ca. 1790–1810. Height 7.375", diameter 8", handle 8.5". Deep-body form with a large gate, heavy triangular-section legs splayed and set well under. Rim has a pouring spout at 90° to the tapering handle.

Cast iron lid may be original to this vessel. It has an inset rim to fit but also a wide beveled edge that could also fit in the flared lip of a pot. The raised rim could also hold hot coals as a Dutch oven lid. Skillets were marketed with and without lids. Diameter 9".

Skillet, cast iron, American, ca. 1800–1820. Height 5.5", diameter 6.5", handle 6.25". A rounded body form typical of the late eighteenth and early nineteenth centuries.[21] Rounded triangular-section legs 1/3 worn away, tapered handle.

Bottom with rounded triangular section legs and a gate.

Skillet, cast iron, American, ca. 1800–1820. Height 4.375", diameter 5", handle 5.25". D-section legs worn away, tapered handle.

Bottom with D-shaped legs and a gate.

Skillet, cast iron, American, ca. 1850–1900. Height 3.5", diameter 5", handle 4.375". A small vessel for use on a stove top having a rounded body with triangular-stub feet. Gate on the bottom.

Teardrop handle is of the early thin type and has a chevron-shaped pad where it joins the body. A pouring spout indicated use for preparing sauces.

Teardrop handle typical of this period marked "7 ins".

Skillet, cast iron, tin, American, ca. 1840–1860. Height 5.5", diameter 7", handle 5.625". Angular form. Tin lid.

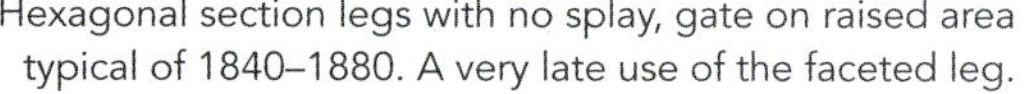

Hexagonal section legs with no splay, gate on raised area typical of 1840–1880. A very late use of the faceted leg.

TOP to BOTTOM:

Two fry pans/spiders, cast iron, American, ca. 1800. Miniature fry pan on left height 1.875", diameter 3.5". Delicate D-section handle, possibly a sales sample or toy. Large pan on right height 4.5", diameter 11.5", handle 7". Delicate D-section legs, tapered handle, long-thin gate.

Large pan is marked "WL" in an oval cartouche on side. Possibly made by William Lewis at Hope Furnace, Lewistown, Pennsylvania, built in 1798.[22]

Bottom of "WL" pan, gate on bottom, D-section legs.

Hanging fry pan, cast iron, American, ca. 1790–1820. Diameter 11.5". This flat-bottomed pan with D-section legs and a bail that swivels side to side has a pouring spout. In use, it could hang over a fire or stand on the hearth over coals. Thick gate on the bottom.

LEFT to RIGHT:

Hanging fry pan, cast iron, wrought iron, English, ca. 1827–1880. Diameter 12.75", depth 2". A very thin casting with a wrought iron fixed handle having a fixed loop at the top for hanging. The handle is set so as to make pouring easy, hence the arch over the spout. Long-thin gate on the bottom.

Marked on the bottom "A. KENRICK & SONS 10 1/2 Inch". Archibald Kenrick was a prolific maker of cast iron holloware in West Bromwich, England, beginning in 1791.[23] Cast iron porringers are the most frequently seen Kenrick products.

Marked on the tapered handle with a loop at the end "G. W. IBACH". Gustav William Ibach, born in 1791, was one of five sons of Frederick William Ibach, a native of Germany who immigrated to Philadelphia in 1796. The family were blacksmiths who worked in Berks and Lehigh counties.[24]

Skillet/Spider, wrought iron, American, ca. 1810–1830. Diameter 8.5", handle 11.75". This round-bottom blacksmith-made form is peculiar to Pennsylvania. Heavily used and eroded body has holes. Legs are restored.

LEFT to RIGHT:

Spider, cast iron, American, ca. 1840–1860. Diameter 10.5", handle 5.25". Round-bottom form with stub feet. Inset rim for a lid. Flat teardrop handle projects from the top of the rim and has no hole. This is the final form of the spider or round-bottom skillet.

Marked on the bottom "9 1/2". This thin casting with a long gate was used over an open stove-lid hole as can be seen by the fire erosion on the bottom.

Spider, cast iron, American, ca. 1840–1860. Diameter 8.25". Round bottom with stub feet. Inset rim for a lid. Flat teardrop handle with no hole projects from the rim. This is a smaller version of the previous sample.

Spider, cast iron, American, ca. 1840–1860. Diameter 5". A small vessel with a slightly rounded bottom for stove top use. Stub feet, gate on the bottom. The teardrop handle is now arched and has a pointed end with a round hole.

Fry pan, cast iron, American, ca. 1830–1850. Diameter 11.5", handle 8.25". Handle with molded edges and a hole.

This heavy casting is raised on short feet so as to clear the projecting gate on the bottom. This is an early pan made before gates could be broken off close to the bottom surface.

Bottom has a foot rim (which is sometimes called a smoke ring) to clear the long-thin gate. This is a light, very smooth casting typical of the period 1860–1890, the apogee of casting perfection.

Fry pan, cast iron, American, ca. 1860–1880. Diameter 11.75", handle 5". Two pouring spouts at 90^{0} to the handle on opposite sides. Pointed teardrop handle slightly raised from the rim with an elongated hole. Raised moldings on inside edges of the handle and number "10".

Fry pan, cast iron, American, ca. 1890–1910. Diameter 13", handle 5.5". Hollowed-arched handle with rounded end and teardrop-shaped hole, marked "10". Shallow-pouring spout. Lathe turned on the inside.

Bottom has a raised foot rim and a long-thin gate. Marked "MARIETTA PA R & Co. 10 IN". This may be a product of the Marietta Casting Co. or the Marietta Hollow Ware and Enameling Co. Both are listed in the *Thomas Register Buyer's Guide* in 1905, and in the 1890 *Cyclopedia of Manufactures*.[25]

Fry pan, cast iron, American, ca. 1880–1910. Diameter 4.875". Flat-blunt teardrop handle with an elongated hole and hollowed underside. A small pan with a pouring spout. The gate, ground off, was on the side of the handle. Gates were now usually on the rim, leaving the bottom flat, enabling it to fully contact the stove top or burner.

Griddle, cast iron, American, ca. 1750. Diameter 11.75", handle 12.5". Triangular-section legs worn to stubs, gate on the bottom. A very heavy casting with a 1" raised rim. Handle tapers to a circular pad with an heart-shaped opening. Used heavily long enough for the front to become badly fire eroded. This is a primitive casting.

Griddle, cast iron, American, ca. 1770–1780. Diameter 9.75". Heavy triangular-section legs, the front legs worn so as to slope the plate. Legs have traces of a fillet where they join the plate, a feature of some Pine Grove pots. Double fluted handle ends in an open circle.

Griddle, cast iron, American, ca. 1780–1810. Diameter 12.25", handle 10.5". Gate on the bottom. Reeded handle in the form of a column with a base and suggestion of an ionic capital in the form of an open heart. This refined casting owes its decorative features to Federal period classical motifs.

Octagonal section legs are unusual for this period.

Griddle or Bake Plate, cast iron, wrought iron American, ca. 1800–1830. Diameter 12.5", handle 9.5". This griddle, often called a bake plate by early furnace operators, was cast without legs for use on a stove or on a trivet over a fire. Gate under the handle base.

The open teardrop handle with a simple incised line decoration is a precursor of 1840–1880 skillet and fry-pan handles.

Trivets, wrought iron, ca. 1700–1800. Round trivet diameter 8.5", height 9.5". Triangular trivet 12.5" each side, height 9".

Griddle or Bake Plate, cast iron, American, ca. 1820–1840. Diameter 12.75". Intended for stove top use, this griddle has a gate on its edge, leaving the bottom free of any raised area. The rectangular handle is also found on eighteenth century examples, but is here angled up so as to be easily gripped when on a stove top.

Hanging griddle, cast iron, wrought iron, American, ca. 1750–1800. Diameter 11", hanging arm 20.5". Cast plate with triangular-section legs, gate on the bottom. A tapering wrought iron arm with chamfered edges raised to a well-formed swivel with a large button. The arm is tenoned through a rectangular extension to the side of the plate and peened over into another large button. Hanging griddles with legs are rare.

Chapter 8

MORTARS

Cast iron mortars were among the early products of American furnaces. They were among the castings noted at Braintree furnace in 1647.1 Pestles were wrought iron forged by the furnace blacksmith. Later pestles were of cast iron. Since the mortar bottom had to be perfectly flat to be stable for grinding, sprues were cut and ground off flush. Gates often were at the side. Chinese mortars are cast by pouring iron into the open mould, leaving the bottom with a pocked appearance. (See page 146.)

Forms varied but often took the tapered form of a drinking tumbler, tapering into the bottom. Tops flared out with a molded edge, as did the bases. Eighteenth century moldings were more elaborate than those of the nineteenth century. (Compare pages 144 and 145.)

Usually seventeenth century forms tended towards the tall and narrow. Eighteenth century mortars were still tall but wider in proportion to the height. (See below.) Nineteenth century examples look more squat. A comparison of actual lip diameter and height measurements shows that most mortars are actually wider than they are tall. Late nineteenth century examples are lighter and frequently of an urn shape.[2]

Mortar handles take the form of a bone-like projection on opposite sides or a rectangular ear-like projection. On those having handles, the molds usually were in two halves vertically with the parting line through the handles. Those cast without handles used molds parting at the narrowest diameter near the base or at the beginning of the molding. Earliest examples may have been molded in baked loam as were pots; later mortars were molded and cast in sand molds.

Iron pestles were generally simpler than bronze types, and some of the earliest were forged of wrought iron. Those of cast iron were cast in halves in sand molds parting longitudinally and will show a seam mark along their length on either side. (See page 145.)

Mortar, cast iron, American, ca. 1650–1730. Diameter at lip 8", height 7.25", pestle, wrought iron, length 12". A narrow-bodied form with a wide flaring lip and a crudely formed off-center base. This mortar is probably from an early furnace. It appears to have been cast in a loam mold although no parting seams are visible on the heavily rusted surface. It has a wide, shallowly molded area around the underside of the lip. The pestle is blacksmith forged.

Mortar, cast iron, American, ca. 1750–1790. Diameter at the lip 7.5", height 7.375". Pestle, wrought iron, length 12". Flask-cast in a sand mold. Wider in proportion to height than the earlier example. This mortar has a cyma-recta molding combined with a cove under the lip and a cove, step, and ogee molding on the base. These moldings, typical of the eighteenth century, are more elaborate than those of the nineteenth century. The smith-made pestle appears worn away where it contacts the mortar wall.

Mortar, cast iron, American, ca. 1780–1820. Diameter at the lip 7.875", height 7.375". Pestle, cast iron, 11.75" long. A wider form with narrower lip, this mortar was cast in a flask in a sand mold. The gate is at the side of the bottom molding. The lip molding is comprised of two ovulo or quarter rounds. The base molding has an ovulo and a step. The pestle is cast iron with the parting line running its length. It appears to be later than the mortar and has the number "7" cast on it.

Mortars, cast iron, American, ca. 1760–1800. Left diameter at the lip 13", height 12". Right diameter at the lip 4.5", height 4". Both were cast in two-part molds parting vertically through the ears and have gates on the base moldings. Moldings are in the eighteenth-century style. The large mortar was found near Hagerstown, Maryland, and may have been cast at the Mt. Aetna furnace. The smaller example has an ear style found as early as the sixteenth century.[3]

The larger mortar was made by Miles Greenwood, who operated a foundry in Cincinnati, Ohio, from 1836–1885.[4] The pestle is marked "GREENWOOD".

Mortars, cast iron, American, ca. 1840–1870. Left diameter at the lip 9", height 7.375". Pestle, cast iron, length 12.5". Right diameter at the lip 4", height 3.5". Pestle, cast iron, length 6". With both top and bottom moldings composed of cove and quarter round, these wide, low mortars are typical of the nineteenth century. The larger has a ground-off sprue, the smaller has a gate. Both are located on the bottom of the mortars.

Mortar, cast iron, Chinese, ca. 1750–1850, diameter at lip 4.75", height 7". Pestle, cast iron, wooden T-handle, length 12.5". This mortar has a typical Chinese vase form and is similarly shaped within. Cast in a two-part mold with the bottom up and open. There is no sprue or gate, the iron having been ladled directly into the open mold, which was probably of loam. The design was scratched free hand onto the moist clay of the wall thickness prior to the application of the outer layer, which then reproduced the design.

The bottom, cast open to the air, shows cavities where the molten iron bubbled prior to cooling.

Chapter 9

REPAIRS AND CLEANING, MISCELLANEOUS HOLLOWARE, AND CONCLUDING REMARKS

Although cast iron vessels may seem to be impossible or unlikely to be repaired, they were in early times of enough value to make the effort worthwhile. Repairs were usually a wrought iron hoop or band around the vessel at the rim to draw closed a crack or by the insertion of a foot, made by using wrought iron. The Chinese had a method for actually casting in a patch on cast vessels, but their way was unknown in America.[1]

Repairs were generally the work of the local blacksmith. Matthew Patton of Bedford, New Hampshire, and his family were apparently rough on pots. His diary has numerous entries detailing pot repairs by different blacksmiths:

> March 13, 1758 ... James Kennedy hooped a pot for me with two hoops.[2]
>
> December 22, 1762 I went to John Jacobs and got one new shoe made of my iron and 4 shoes set and a foot put into a pot.[3]
>
> December 13 & 14, 1764 I got 2 pots mended with each a foot and a beal (bail) and my mare shod...[4]

Collecting Holloware

When buying antique holloware, be especially careful and wary of painted examples. A slight bulge or irregularity under paint may hide an epoxy repair of a crack or hole. More cleverly done epoxy repairs may be very hard to see. Unlike holes plugged with copper rivets or modern welded repairs, epoxy will not stand up to use over a fire.

Modern welding techniques enable the repairing of cast iron in ways not possible in the past. Legs may be reconstructed and cracks sealed. The newness of a weld may be covered with paint, but it is very difficult to produce rust that matches the old iron. New metal rusts to an orange color rather than the brown of the older surface and pitting will not match either.

Small holes and casting imperfections were plugged with copper rivets or slivers. These may have been done at the furnace so as to be able to sell an otherwise unmarketable piece. These repairs generally have held up well and do not lessen the value of a pot. Pots used for growing flowers and having holes drilled for drainage in the bottom may be worth preserving, but plugging the holes may result in cracking the pot made brittle by deep rust pitting.

A frequently used form of repair was effected at the furnace soon after a piece was cast. If the casting was found to be porous, having one or more holes extending to the inside so as to let fluid out, these could be plugged with soft copper rivets driven into the holes. (See page 38.) Once hammered in and peened over, these plugs would expand and contract with the pot as heat was applied or cooling occurred and remained tight.

Repairing a broken out foot was an involved process, the results of which were probably never truly satisfactory. The smith would forge a foot from wrought iron and lock it to the pot interior with a washer shaped to fit the pot's curves. A slot in the foot with a tapered pin would clamp another washer to the pot exterior and lock the foot in place. The chances of this repair being leak-free were remote. Swinging a heavy loaded pot off a trammel or hook could be tricky. If it collided with another pot it might crack. If set down roughly on a stone hearth, a leg might be driven inward and broken. We will never know how many soups and stews ended up splashed across the romantically fabled hearth.

When cleaning antique holloware, use water soluble paint remover to strip paint from a pot, taking care to protect eyes and skin. Wash the pot with dish detergent and thoroughly rinse with clean water. After the paint is removed, any remaining rust may be lifted with a hand or power wire brush. Baked on soot from long use over an open fire will have to be removed by chipping with a dull knife since paint remover will not touch it.

Rust by itself can be removed with a power wire brush. This will create a lot of dust, so a mask and eye protection are in order. Under no circumstances should any old cast iron piece be sand blasted. This will result in a pitted, grey surface that can never be restored. Do not use fine steel wool, which will leave tiny flecks of metal behind, nor graphite, which is virtually impossible to remove from a pot.

Once the major rust has been removed, simmer a vinegar and water solution in the pot to remove any lingering impurities. After the vinegar solution cools, rinse the pot well with water, and then simmer a dish washing liquid and water solution in the pot to neutralize the remaining vinegar and to continue to clean the pot. After the pot cools, rinse well with water and scrub it with a stainless steel scrubbing pad in a dishwashing solution, then rinse and dry the pot. To prevent rust, rub the surface lightly with mineral oil and wipe off the excess. Eventually, use over the fire will result in a lustrous black finish. (See page 31, top.)

Pots that will not be used for cooking may be treated by applying a 50/50 mixture of boiled linseed oil and mineral spirits, then wiping off all the excess. Not removing the excess will result in a sticky, gummy surface that will be hard to remove. Do not coat pots with motor oil or similar products.

If a pot is not going to be used for cooking and the color is not acceptable, hang it over an open fire so that soot builds up on the surface. Periodically polish the surface with a soft cloth. As a last resort, spray lightly with a barbecue black paint and wipe off before it dries fully. This will give a little color with some surface showing through. After twenty-four hours, when fully dry, apply and wipe off the linseed oil and mineral spirits mixture.

A more permanent rust inhibiting preservation method is used by museums where heavily rusted archaeologically recovered artifacts are displayed. Rust and scale are removed by electrolysis, a process that may take days or weeks, then dried and coated with beeswax brushed on as a hot liquid. This seals the iron and prevents further deterioration. Although well-preserved, artifacts treated in this way appear to be coated and do not retain anything like the original surface appearance. A pot that has been excavated requires this treatment to arrest the rusting process.

LEFT to RIGHT:

Bowl, cast iron, American, ca. 1650–1720. Diameter 5.75", height 2". With lobed gadrooning around its circumference, this heavily cast bowl reflects the Mannerist style of the sixteenth and early seventeenth centuries. Such items may have been made by ironworkers at early ironworks as special gifts, but are not typical of everyday production.

The bowl has a sprue on the bottom within a low foot rim.

Oil lamp, cast iron, American, ca. 1650–1750. Diameter 5", height 2.5". Sprue on the bottom. Four short tapered round-section legs. A thickened rim with a semi-circular notch would receive a wick, which lay in the oil. Lamps burning fish oil were used in coastal areas of early New England.

Basin, cast iron, American, ca. 1820–1840. Diameter at rim 12.75", height to rim 3.5". Flask cast with a gate and three stub pads on the bottom. Although it has no handle or ears for a bail, making it difficult to move when hot, buildup of carbon from wood fires adhering to the bottom indicates use over an open stove hole, perhaps to heat water for some washing purpose. Rust on the interior suggests use with water alone as opposed to food preparation, which results in a greasy surface.

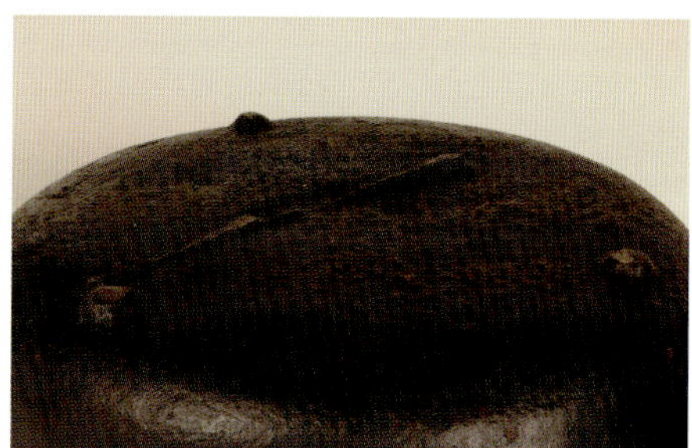

Three stub pads on the bottom provide stability when this vessel is set on a table or stove top.

Hanging kettle or pan, cast iron, American, ca. 1820–1840. Diameter at rim 13", height to rim 3.5". Flask cast using a gate. The square-section bail attached to New England style ears raised from the rim has a swiveling hook at the top for use over an open fire.

Hanging kettle or pan, American, ca. 1840–1860. Diameter at rim 9.75". height to rim 3". Three short, triangular feet and a gate on the bottom. Ears for bail extend out and up from the rim, enabling use of a now missing lid. Ears have a ledge preventing the bail from contact with a hot stove top when in use over an open stove hole.

Cup and saucer, cast iron, American, ca. 1790–1850. This crudely cast cup and associated saucer were found in New Hampshire. Cup diameter 2.75", height 2.5". The cup is marked "T H & Co". It was cast in a two-part mold parting vertically through the handle and has a gate on the bottom.

The saucer diameter is 5.75". It has a slightly lobed inner surface and was cast with a sprue. It may be older than the cup. Cast iron ware was often made for institutional use.

LEFT to RIGHT:

Broiler pan, cast iron, American, ca. 1849. 7" x 12.25" x 2.5". Made at Haag, Kline & Co. foundry in Bernville, Pennsylvania, to a pattern made by Peter Derr, who is better known for smith-made Betty lamps and kitchen utensils.[5]

Cast-in mark "P. DERR" on underside was incised in the wooden pattern.

Ebelskiver (apple pancake balls) pan, cast iron, American, ca. 1840–1850. Length with handle 10.75", height 2.75". Seven rounded cups hold pancake batter, which is browned and rotated around a piece of apple to form a ball. Teardrop handle with teardrop hole and hollowed back. A heavy casting.

Bottom showing four D-section legs with chamfered back corners and a sprue.

Included here are some interesting holloware items that do not strictly fit into the previous chapters. The early bowl and oil lamp were found at an antique co-op flea market. The bowl was not identified in any way and the lamp was labeled as a ladle. The writer has found throughout his collecting career that early and interesting cast iron may turn up anywhere from yard sales, shops, flea markets, and auctions to antique shows. Many pieces are not readily identified and are not valued the same as easily recognized antiques.

On the other hand, a piece such as the cast iron broiler pan molded by Peter Derr and bearing his name cast in the bottom is bound to be costly. The example shown is very rare and came from a well-known collection. One need not have deep pockets to afford most of these items. Now and then, a unique or significant piece will be worth stretching to acquire.

The book was written to fill a perceived need for a source of information on holloware of the years before 1900. Where possible, facts are documented, but many statements are based on changes of details noted over forty years of collecting. This is a preliminary study to which others will hopefully add corrections and information in the coming years.

Early holloware is still waiting to be discovered; learn to recognize it. Successful hunting!

ENDNOTES

Chapter 1

1. Leslie Aitchison. *A History of Metals*, V. 1, pp. 76, 155.
2. Ibid., 40–41.
3. Ibid., 121.
4. J. Seymour Lindsay. *Iron and Brass Implements of the English House*, p. 25, Figs. 108, 109.
5. William W. Fitzhugh and Elizabeth A. Ward, eds. *Vikings The North Atlantic Saga*, p. 158, Fig. 10.5. Paul B. DuChaillu. *The Viking Age*, V. 2, p. 151, Fig. 931.
6. Hanns-Ulrich Haedeke. *Metalwork*, p. 65.
7. Aitchison. *Metals*, V. 2, p. 326.
8. Charles Singer, E. J. Holmyard, and A. R. Hall, eds. *A History of Technology*, V. 1, p. 634.
9. Ibid., p. 629.
10. Haedeke. *Metalwork*, p. 65.
11. Raymond Lister. *Decorative Cast Ironwork in Great Britain*, p. 40–42.
12. Haedeke. *Metalwork*, p. 67. Roderick Butler and Christopher Green. *English Bronze Cooking Vessels and Their Founders 1350–1830*, pp. 22–27.
13. Francis Parkman. *The Discovery of the Great West*, p. 242.
14. F. W. Robins. *The Smith*, p. 17.
15. Singer, Holmyard, and Hall. *History of Technology*, V. 2, p. 475.
16. Butler and Green. *English Bronze Cooking Vessels and Their Founders 1350–1830*, p. 27.
17. DuChaillu. *Viking Age*, V. 1, p. 148, Fig. 246.
18. Haedeke. *Metalwork*, p. 65–67.
19. Onno ter Kuile. *Koper & Brons*, p. 189, pl. 263.
20. Ibid., p. 190, pl. 265.
21. Haedeke. *Metalwork*, p. 68. ter Kuile, p. 197, pl. 274.
22. Jost Amman and Hans Sachs. *The Book of Trades*, p. 62. Raymond Lecog. *Les Objets de la Vie Domestique*, p. 127.
23. Butler and Green. *English Bronze Cooking Vessels and Their Founders 1350–1830*, pp. 114–115.
24. Ibid., pp. 71–72, 188.
25. Haedeke. *Metalwork*, p. 56.
26. Rachael Feild. *Irons in the Fire*, p. 77.
27. Butler and Green. *English Bronze Cooking Vessels and Their Founders 1350–1830*, p. 128.
28. Henry J. Kaufman. *American Copper & Brass*, pp. 21–23.

Chapter 2

1. Luigi Nessi. *Antique Tools and Instruments*, p. 216, Fig. 84.
2. Robert B. Gordon. *American Iron 1607–1900*, p. 14.
3. Singer, Holmyand, and Hall. *History of Technology, V. 1*, 596.
4. H. R. Schubert. *History of the British Iron and Steel Industry*, p. 163.
5. Fitzhugh and Ward. *Vikings*, pp. 158–159.

Chapter 3

1. Gordon. *American Iron 1607–1900*, p. 100.
2. Donald B. Wagner. *Ferrous Metallurgy*, pp. 356–357.
3. James M. Swank. *History of the Manufacture of Iron in All Ages*, p. 25.
4. Schubert. *British Iron and Steel*, p. 163.
5. Ibid., p. 268.
6. Rene Antoine Ferchault Reaumur. *The Art of Converting Wrought Iron into Steel & The Art of Making Cast Iron Malleable*, p. 351.
7. E. N. Hartley. *Ironworks on the Saugus*, pp. 109, 127.
8. Ibid., p. 127; Swank, *Iron in All Ages*, p. 113.
9. Susan Geib. *Hammersmith: The Saugus Ironworks as an Example of Early Industrialism*, p. 354.
10. Arthur Raistrick. *Dynasty of Iron-Founders*, p. 22.
11. Denis Diderot. *Encyclopédie, ou Dictionaire Raisonne des Sciences, des Arts, et des Métiers*, Forges Sec. III plts. 3, 4.
12. Raistrick. *Dynasty*, p. 21.
13. Edward H. Knight. *Knight's American Mechanical Dictionary*, V. 1, p. 533.
14. Raistrick. *Dynasty*, p. 280.
15. Pine Grove Furnace. *Waste Book*, 1786.
16. David Bremner. *The Industries of Scotland*, pp. 44–46.
17. Raistrick. *Dynasty*, 45; William Byrd. *A Journey to the Land of Eden and Other Papers*, p. 356.
18. Byrd. *A Journey*, p. 358.
19. Leander Bishop. *A History of American Manufactures from 1608 to 1860*, V. I, p. 484.
20. Ibid.
21. Gordon. *American Iron*, p. 28.
22. Estelle Cremers. *Reading Furnace 1736*, pp. 147, 149.
23. Susan Winter Frye. *Archeological Excavations at the Antietam Iron Furnace Complex*, pp. 108–109.
24. Raistrick. *Dynasty*, p. 15.
25. Ibid., p. 283.
26. Bremner. *Industries of Scotland*, p. 44.
27. Lewis Burd Walker, ed. *The Burd Papers*, pp. 137, 140.
28. Arthur D. Pierce. *Iron in the Pines*, pp. 121–126.
29. Richard L. Tritt and Randy Watts, eds. *At A Place Called The Boiling Springs*, p. 48.
30. Swank. *Iron in All Ages*, p. 188.
31. Alfred Gemmell. *The Charcoal Iron Industry of the Perkiomen Valley*, p. 34.
32. John Bivens, Jr. "Isaac Zane and the Products of Marlboro Furnace." *Journal of Early Southern Decorative Arts* 11, no. 1 (1985): p. 33.
33. Pine Grove Furnace. *Waste Book*, July 1, 1786.
34. Pine Grove Furnace. *Day Book*, July 12, 1825.
35. Willis W. Eisenhart. *A History of Abbottstown*, p. 26.
36. Berwick Twp., Adams Co., Pa., *Tax List*, 1825.
37. Convention of Ironmasters. *Documents Relating to the Manufacture of Iron in Pennsylvania*, 1850.
38. Gemmell. *Charcoal Iron*, p. 104.
39. Swank. *Iron in All Ages*, p. 111.
40. Fredrika A. Burrows. *Cannonballs & Cranberries*, p. 34; William Bartlett Murdock. *Blast Furnaces of Carver*, pp. 16, 20. Tom Kelleher, Curator, Old Sturbridge Village. *Email*, 8/12/2010.
41. Brian Bracegirdle and Patricia H. Miles. *The Darbys and the Ironbridge Gorge*, p. 10.
42. Ibid.
43. Frye. *Archeological Excavations*, p. 106
44. Ibid., p. 53.
45. Lenore Embrick Flower. *History of Pine Grove Furnace*, p. 31.
46. *The Plymouth County Directory and Historical Register of the Old Colony*, 1867.
47. Nicholas B. Wainwright. *Philadelphia in the Romantic Age of Lithography*, p. 239.
48. Donald L. Fennimore. *Iron at Winterthur*, p. 32.
49. Ibid., p. 94.
50. Edwin T. Freedley. *Philadelphia and its Manufactures, etc.*, p. 291.
51. Ibid., p. 499.
52. Tammis Kane Groft. *Cast With Style*, p. 85.
53. Ibid., p. 15.
54. Ibid., pp. 105, 112; William Woys Weaver. *America Eats*, p.188.
55. J. P. Lesley. *The Iron Manufacturer's Guide*, p. 39.
56. Dover Stamping Company. *Trade Catalog*, p. 132.
57. *The Manufactories and Manufacturers of Pennsylvania*, p. 510.
58. David G. Smith and Chuck Wafford. *The Book Of Griswold and Wagner*, p. 75.

59. Fennimore. *Iron At Winterthur*, p. 96.
60. Barbara Israel. *Antique Garden Ornament*, p. 217.
61. R. H. Campbell. *Carron Company*, p. 35.
62. Ibid., p. 72.
63. Israel. *Antique Garden Ornament*, p. 219.
64. Pine Grove Furnace. *Ware Book 1814*, p. 7.
65. Jeffery P. Brian. *Tunica Treasure*, p. 138.
66. Richard Veit and Charles Bello. "Contact and Early Historic Period Archaeology in the Delaware Valley", pp. 109–110.
67. Henry-Rene D'Allemagne. *Musée Le Secq des Tournelles à Rouen Ferronnerie*, V. 2, pl. CCCXLVI; Marian Campbell. *Decorative Ironwork*, 83; Le Cog. *Les Objets*, p. 172.
68. John D. Tyler. "Cast Iron Cooking Vessels," *The Magazine Antiques*, (August 1971), p. 221.

Chapter 4

1. *Oxford English Dictionary*, 1961, s. v. "Kettle".
2. Butler and Green. *English Bronze Cooking Vessels ...*, p. 27.
3. Lister. *Decorative Cast Ironwork*, pp. 40-42.
4. Harry Miller. *Canada's Historic First Iron Castings*, pp. 11–12; Rita Susswein Gottesman, ed. *The Arts and Crafts in New York 1777–1799*, p. 241.
5. Richard Barons, ed. *The American Hearth*, 19; Susan G. Gibson, ed. *Burr's Hill: A 17th Century Wampannog Burial Ground in Warren, Rhode Island*, p. 139.
6. John Warner Barber. *Connecticut Historical Collections*, p. 555; Charles Rufus Harte. *Connecticut's Cannon*, pp. 8–10; Philip M. Isaacson. *The American Eagle*, pp. 26, 38; Adam Ward Rome. *Connecticut's Cannon: The Salisbury Furnace in the American Revolution*, p. 24.
7. Ed Kirby. *Echoes of Iron*, p. 7.
8. Jane C. Nylander. *Our Own Snug Fireside*, p. 62.
9. Linda Campbell Franklin. *300 Years of Kitchen Collectibles*, p. 444; Joseph E. Walker. *Hopewell Village*, p. 153; Weaver, *America Eats*, p. 150.
10. Marc Harris. "John Wilkeson" in *Iron and Steel in the Nineteenth Century*, ed. Paul F. Paskoff (New York: Facts on File, 1989, pp. 367–368).
11. Weaver. *America Eats*, pp. 150–151.
12. Smith and Wafford. *Griswold and Wagner*, p. 247.
13. Le Cog. *Les Objets*, pp. 172–173.

Chapter 5

1. Pine Grove Furnace. *Ware Book*, 1814, p. 1
2. Barons. *The American Hearth*, p. 26.
3. John J. Ragsdale. *Dutch Ovens Chronicled*, p. 13.
4. Pine Grove Furnace. *Waste Book*, 1786.
5. Rev. Charles, D. D. Elliot. *The Life of the Rev. Robert R. Roberts*, 81; Ragsdale. *Dutch Ovens*, p. 29.
6. Ragsdale. *Dutch Ovens*, pp. 14–15.
7. Laurel Furnace. *Account Book*, 6 Oct., 1801.
8. Franklin. *Kitchen Collectibles*, p. 444; Smith and Wafford. *Griswold and Wagner*, p. 63.
9. Berkshire Furnace. *Ledger*, Feb. 24, 1784; Pierce. *Iron in the Pines*, p. 122.
10. Ragsdale. *Dutch Ovens*, p. 67.
11. Pierce. *Iron in the Pines*, p. 122; Suzanne Fellman Jacob. *The History of Joanna Furnace 1791–1999*, p. 285.

Chapter 6

1. Bishop. *History of American Manufactures*, V. I, p. 488.
2. Ibid., V. 3, p. 492.
3. Pine Grove Furnace. *Waste Book*, 1786.
4. Tritt and Watts. *At a Place Called The Boiling Springs*, p. 48.
5. Franklin. *Kitchen Collectibles*, p. 547.
6. Henry C. Mercer. *The Bible in Iron*, p. 248; Clyde A. Sanders and Dudley C. Gould. *History Cast in Metal*, p. 12.
7. Merri Lou Scribner Schaumann. *Taverns of Cumberland County Pennsylvania 1750–1840*, p. 166.
8. Bishop. *History of American Manufactures*, V. III, p. 203.
9. Franklin. *Kitchen Collectibles*, p. 547.
10. Bishop. *History of American Manufactures*, V. III, p. 203.
11. Dover Stamping Company. *Trade Catalog*, p. 133.
12. Wainwright. *Philadelphia Romantic Lithography*, p. 97.
13. Freedley. *Philadelphia and its Manufactures*, p. 292.
14. Bishop. *History of American Manufactures*, V. III, p. 492.
15. Groft. *Cast With Style*, p. 112.
16. Ibid., pp. 106, 117.
17. Franklin. *Kitchen Collectibles*, p. 547.
18. Smith and Wafford. *Griswold and Wagner*, p. 78.
19. Feild. *Irons in the Fire*, p. 97.

Chapter 7

1. Butler and Green. *English Bronze Cooking Vessels*, p. 9.
2. Ibid., p. 10.
3. *Webster's International Dictionary*, 1898, s. v. "Spider."
4. Arthur Cecil Bining, PHD. *Pennsylvania Iron Manufacture in the Eighteenth Century*, p. 191.
5. Laurel Furnace. *Account Book*, 1804.
6. Pine Grove Furnace. *Ware Book*, 1814, pp. 3–4.
7. James S. Brown. *Allaire's Lost Empire*, p. 57.
8. John Russell Bartlett. *Dictionary of Americanisms*, p. 434.
9. Dover Stamping Co. *Trade Catalog*, p. 133.
10. Smith and Wafford. *Griswold and Wagner*, p. 15.
11. Mary Ann Furnace. *Note Book*, 1850.
12. Feild. *Irons in the Fire*, p. 247.
13. Jeannette Lasansky. *To Draw, Upset and Weld*, p. 45.
14. Elizabeth Melling. *Kentish Sources V Some Kentish Houses*, p. 22.
15. Nancy Carlisle and Melinda Nasardinov. *America's Kitchens*, p. 31.
16. Jacob. *The History of Joanna Furnace 1791–1999*, p. 285.
17. Smith and Wafford. *Griswold and Wagner*, p. 53.
18. Geib. *Hammersmith*, p. 354.
19. Swank. *Iron in all Ages*, p. 113; Hartley. *Ironworks on the Saugus*, p. 127.
20. Edward F. Heite. *The Pioneer Phase of the Chesapeake Iron Industry*, p. 138; William Byrd. *Journey to the Land of Eden*, p. 356.
21. Nina Fletcher Little. *Little by Little*, pp. 30, 34.
22. Swank. *Iron in All Ages*, p. 210.
23. Fennimore. *Iron at Winterthur*, p. 105.
24. Lasansky. *To Draw, Upset and Weld*, p. 44.
25. Franklin. *Kitchen Collectibles*, p. 530.

Chapter 8

1. Swank, p. 113.
2. Smith & Wafford, p. 188.
3. ter Kuile. *Kopper and Brons*, pp. 205-206.
4. Harris in Paskoff, pp. 149-152.

Chapter 9

1. Rudolf P. Hommel. *China at Work*, pp. 31–34.
2. Matthew Patten. *The Diary of Matthew Patten*, p. 49.
3. Ibid., p. 119.
4. Ibid., p. 145.
5. Spears. *The House of Derr*, p. 141

GLOSSARY

Air Furnace: a furnace in which metal is remelted without contacting the fuel.

Back Coping: hollowing on the back of a pattern so as to use less metal when cast.

Bail: the handle of a pot, kettle, or teakettle, usually forged by a blacksmith and not cast.

Blast Furnace: a furnace where iron ore is reduced to a molten state and cast into molds or billets (pigs).

Bloomery: a forge fired with charcoal in which iron ore was reduced to wrought iron in the form of a pasty lump known as a bloom, which was then hammered to form a bar. Some slag was forced out of the semi-molten bloom during the hammering process. The remaining slag formed long inclusions in the iron, giving it a fibrous appearance (also see forge).

Bog Ore: iron ore precipitated by iron-rich groundwater with the aid of bacteria in bogs or wetlands.

Brass: an alloy of copper and calamine or zinc.

Brazed: iron, brass, bronze, or copper jointed by a molten brass alloy.

Bronze: an alloy of copper and tin, sometimes containing lead.

Bulge Pot: a cylindrical but slightly bulged-out type of vessel typical of the late nineteenth century.

Cast Iron: iron smelted from ore in a blast furnace or remelted from pig iron or scrap iron in a foundry and poured in molten form into a mold, where it will solidify.

Cheek(s): the two semi-cylindrical halves of a cast iron mold used to cast pots.

Core: the interior mold for cast holloware or for any casting having a hollow center.

Cupola: a tall, iron-jacketed cylindrical furnace lined with fire brick wherein cast iron is remelted and then cast into holloware, etc. Small foundries using a cupola with the air blast powered by a steam engine were located in many towns after 1830.

Dutch Oven: a flat-sided, kettle-like form wider than high with long legs to stand over hot coals and a lid with a raised edge flange to hold hot coals. Baking takes place inside between the two fires.

Ears: rounded or angular protrusions on opposite sides near the rim of a pot or kettle used as finger holds or for attaching a bail for lifting.

Fireback: a flat cast iron slab with one decorated side used against the back wall of a fireplace to protect the stone or brick from erosion from the fire. It also reflects heat into the room.

Fish Kettle: a deep, long, and nearly oval vessel on four long legs for use over coals with or without a lid to cook fish.

Flask: a wooden multi-part box filled with molding sand in which various iron articles are cast.

Foot/leg: one of three or four tapered and elongated pins extending downward from the vessel bottom and upon which it stands above coals on the hearth.

Forge: a hearth where wrought iron was produced from raw ore, sometimes called a bloomery since the lump of wrought iron produced was called a bloom. The same sort of forge was used to remelt cast iron pigs from the blast furnace in order to refine them into wrought iron. The first method is called the direct and the second the indirect process. Both used heavy water-powered hammers to shape the iron while physically beating slag out of it. The product of both methods was called wrought iron.

Fry Pan: a wide pan with low sides made from wrought iron or cast iron. Both types may have arched handles or handles extending from the rim and legs.

Founder: the worker in charge of the day-to-day operation of a blast furnace.

Foundry: any establishment where metals are cast. In this study a place where cast iron from a blast furnace is remelted and refined for casting into various vessels. The foundry largely supplanted the blast furnace as the source of holloware beginning about 1830.

Gate: the long, narrow slot in a mold through which the molten iron was poured. The opening tapers from wide at the top on the mold surface to narrow where the vessel shape begins.

Kettle: a vessel having tapered or rounded sides with a flat or rounded bottom. It is wider at the rim than at the base.

Lappet: a flat thickening of a vessel wall at the rim where an ear is formed. They are sometimes shield-shaped or otherwise decorative.

Loam mold: a baked clay (loam) mold for casting holloware formed on a rotating spindle or a potter's wheel using wooden templates to shape the moist clay. It has to be broken to remove the vessel once it has been cast.

Lost-wax casting: The most ancient method of casting, wherein the form of the object is built over a clay core in wax. A layer of clay over the wax model then seals it. The wax is then melted out and molten metal is poured into the resulting cavity. When cool, the outer clay is removed as is the inner core, if a pot.

Mascaron: a protruding grotesque mask or face cast in low relief on a vessel side or leg.

Mold: a container, either of baked clay (loam) or of sand within a wooden flask or cast iron cheeks, having within it the cavity made by a pattern, since removed. Iron poured into the mold to fill the cavity forms the cast iron vessel.

Molder: the maker and caster of the mold.

Parting line: the line visible on the exterior of a vessel formed where parts of the mold join.

Pattern: a model of the vessel to be cast. It may be of wood, iron, brass, or pewter, and of one or more pieces to facilitate its removal from the mold prior to casting.

Pig iron: crude cast iron billets produced at a blast furnace.

Posnet: a vessel with the bulbous shape of a pot and with a short handle extending out from the rim.

Pot: a vessel of bulbous form having the opening at the rim narrower than its width. A straight sided vessel tapering in to the top.

Potter: the seventeenth century term for a molder working to make clay (loam) molds.

Riser: a channel, usually of round section similar to a sprue, formed in a mold to allow air to escape as the mold is filled.

Sand casting: production of vessels using a sand filled molding box (flask), as a mold.

Shoulder: the down-sloping upper part of a pot between the rim and its greatest width (the belly).

Skillet: a straight-sided vessel on three legs having a handle extending out near or at the rim. The bottom may be rounded. The body usually flares outward to the rim.

Slag: the cinder or scoria formed by impurities in iron ore combining with a flux (limestone) in the blast furnace or forge.

Smelting: the process of reducing ore to its liquid or semi-liquid metallic state under intense heat.

Spider: a cast iron or wrought iron frying pan with three legs.

Sprue: the tapered, rounded opening through which molten iron is poured into a mold.

Teakettle: a water boiler having a handle and spout, used to heat water to make tea in a teapot, or for other household uses.

Wrought iron: a low-carbon iron produced by direct reduction of ore in a bloomery forge or by the indirect secondary refining of cast iron pigs in a refinery forge. It has a characteristic wood-like fibrous texture due to inclusions of slag, which are elongated as iron bars are drawn out and shaped under a power hammer.

BIBLIOGRAPHY

Aitchison, Leslie. *A History of Metals.* 2 vols. New York, NY: Interscience Publishers, Inc., 1960.

Amman, Jost and Hans Sachs. *The Book of Trades.* New York, N.Y.: Dover Publications, Inc. 1973.

Barber, John Warner. *Connecticut Historical Collections.* New Haven, CT: Durrie & Peck and J. W. Barber, 1836.

Barons, Richard, ed., *The American Hearth.* Binghamton, NY: Broome County Historical Society, 1976.

Bartlett, John Russell. *Dictionary of Americanisms.* Boston, MA: Little, Brown and Company, 1859.

Berkshire Furnace. *Ledger, 1784, Berks County, PA.* Manuscript Group 2, Business Records Collection, Division of Archives and History, Pennsylvania Historical and Museum Commission, Harrisburg, PA.

Berwick Twp., Adams County PA. *Tax List 1825.* Adams County Historical Society, Gettysburg, PA.

Bining, Arthur Cecil, Ph.D. *Pennsylvania Iron Manufacture in the Eighteenth Century.* Harrisburg, PA: Pennsylvania Historical Commission, 1938.

Biringuccio, Vannoccio. *Pirotechnia.* Introduction and Notes by Cyril Stanley Smith, Translated by Martha Teach Gnudi. New York, NY: American Institute of Mining and Metallurgical Engineers, 1943.

Bishop, J. Leander, A.M., M.D. *A History of American Manufactures from 1608 to 1860.* 3 vols., 3rd ed. Philadelphia, PA: Edward Young & Co., 1868.

Bivins, John Jr., "Isaac Zane and the Products of Marlboro Furnace". *Journal of Early Southern Decorative Arts* 11, no. 1 (May 1985).

Bracegirdle, Brian and Patricia H. Miles. *The Darbys and the Ironbridge Gorge.* Newton Abbot, UK: David & Charles, 1974.

Brain, Jeffery P. *Tunica Treasure.* 2 vols. Cambridge, MA: Harvard University, 1979.

Bremner, David. *The Industries of Scotland.* Reprint of 1869 ed. Newton Abbot, UK: David & Charles, 1969).

Brown, James S. *Allaire's Lost Empire.* Freehold, NJ: The Transcript Printing House, 1958.

Burrows, Fredrika A. *Cannonballs &*

Cranberries. Taunton, MA: William S. Sullwold, Publishing, 1976.

Butler, Roderick and Christopher Green. *English Bronze Cooking Vessels & Their Founders 1350–1830.* Honiton, Devon, UK: Roderick and Valentine Butler, 2003.

Byrd, William. *A Journey to the Land of Eden and Other Papers.* New York, NY: The Vanguard Press, 1928.

Campbell, Marian. *Decorative Ironwork.* New York, NY: Harry N. Abrams, Inc., 1997.

Campbell, R. H. *Carron Company.* Edinburgh and London, UK: Oliver and Boyd, 1961.

Carlisle, Nancy and Melinda Talbot Nasardinov. *America's Kitchens.* Boston, MA: Historic New England, 2008.

Convention of Ironmasters. *Documents Relating to the Manufacture of Iron in Pennsylvania.* Philadelphia, PA: Published by the General Committee, 1850.

Cremers, Estelle. *Reading Furnace 1736.* Elverson, PA: Reading Furnace Press, 1986.

D'Allemagne, Henry-Rene. *Musée Le Secq des Tournelles à Rouen Ferronneric Ancienne.* 2 vols. Paris, France: J. Schemit, 1924.

Diderot, Denis. *Encyclopédie, ou Dictionaire Raisonné des Sciences, des Arts, et des Métiers.* 28 vols. Paris France: Braisson, 1751–1776.

Dover Stamping Co. *Trade Catalog,* 1869 reprint. Princeton, NJ: The Pyne Press, 1971.

Du Chaillu, Paul B. 2 vols. *The Viking Age.* New York, NY: Charles Scribner's Sons, 1890.

Elliot, Rev. Charles, D.D. *The Life of Rev. Robert R. Roberts.* New York, NY: G. Lane & C. B. Tippett, 1841.

Eisenhart, Willis W. *A History of Abbottstown.* n.p.: n. pub, 1953.

Feild, Rachael. *Irons In The Fire.* Ramsbury, UK: The Crowood Press, 1984.

Fennimore, Donald L. *Iron At Winterthur.* Winterthur, DE: The Henry Frances duPont Winterthur Museum, 2004.

Fitzhugh, William W. and Elizabeth A. Ward, eds. *Vikings The North Atlantic Saga.* Washington, DC: Smithsonian Institution Press, 2000.

Flower, Lenore Embick. *History of Pine Grove Furnace.* Carlisle, PA: Cumberland County Historical Society, 2003.

Franklin, Linda Campbell. *300 Years of Kitchen Collectibles.* 3rd. ed. Florence, AL: Books Americana, 1991.

Freedley, Edwin T. *Philadelphia and its Manufactures, etc.* Philadelphia, PA: Edward Young, 1859.

Frye, Susan Winter. *Archeological Excavations at the Antietam Iron Furnace Complex (18 WA 288) Washington County, Maryland.* Manuscript Series No. 37. Annapolis, MD: Maryland Historical Trust, 1984.

Geib, Susan. "Hammersmith: The Saugus Ironworks as an Example of Early Industrialism" in *New England Begins,* vol. II, Jonathan L. Fairbanks, ed. Boston, MA: Museum of Fine Arts, 1982.

Gemmell, Alfred. *The Charcoal Iron Industry of the Perkiomen Valley.* Allentown, PA: Hartenstine Printing House, 1949.

Gibson, Susan G., ed. *Burr's Hill: A 17th Century Wampanoag Burial Ground in Warren, Rhode Island.* Providence, RI: Haffenreffer Museum of Anthropology, Brown University, 1980.

Gordon, Robert B. *American Iron 1607–1900.* Baltimore, MD and London: Johns Hopkins University Press, 1996.

Gottesman, Rita Susswein, ed. *The Arts And Crafts In New York 1777–1799.* New York, NY: The New York Historical Society, 1954.

Groft, Tammis Kane. *Cast With Style.* Rev. ed. Albany, NY: Albany Institute of History and Art, 1984.

Haedeke, Hanns-Ulrich. *Metalwork.* New York, NY: Universe Books, 1970.

Harris, Marc. "John Wilkeson" in *Iron and Steel in the Nineteenth Century.* Paul F. Paskoff, ed. New York, NY: Facts on File, 1989.

Harris, Marc: "Miles Greenwood" in *iron and Steel in the Nineteenth Century.* Paul F. Paskoff, ed. New York, NY: Facts on file, 1989.

Harte, Charles Rufus, "Connecticut's Cannon," *58th Annual Report of the Connecticut Society of Civil Engineers.* Hartford, CT: 1942.

Hartley, E. N. *Ironworks on the Saugus.* Norman, OK: University of Oklahoma Press, 1957.

Heite, Edward F. "The Pioneer Phase of the Chesapeake Iron Industry: Naturalization of a Technology." *Quarterly Bulletin Archeological Society of Virginia* 38, no. 3 (Sept. 1983).

Hommel, Rudolf P. *China at Work.* Doylestown, PA: The Bucks County Historical Society, 1937.

Isaacson, Philip M. *The American Eagle.* Boston, MA: The New York Graphic Society, 1975.

Israel, Barbara. *Antique Garden Ornament.* New York, NY: Harry N. Abrams, Inc. 1999.

Jacob, Suzanne Fellman. *The History of Joanna Furnace 1791–1999.* Geigertown, PA: Hay Creek Valley Historical Association, 1999.

Kauffman, Henry J. *American Copper and Brass.* New York, NY: Bonanza Books, 1979.

Kirby, Ed, *Echoes of Iron.* Sharon, CT: Sharon Historical Society, 1998.

Knight, Edward H. *Knight's American Mechanical Dictionary,* 3 vols. Boston, MA: Houghton, Mifflin and Company, 1876.

ter Kuile, Onno. *Koper & Brons.* Amsterdam: Rijksmuseum, 1986.

Lasansky, Jeannette. *To Draw, Upset, & Weld.* Lewisburg, PA: Union County Historical Society, 1980.

Laurel Furnace. *Account Book, 1804–1812.* Fayette County, PA. Manuscript Group 2, Business Records Collection, Division of Archives and History, Pennsylvania Historical and Museum Commission.

Lecog, Raymond. *Les Objets de la vie domestique.* N.p.: Berger-Levrault, 1979.

Lesley, J. P. *The Iron Manufacturers Guide.* New York, NY: John Wiley, Publisher, 1859.

Lister, Raymond. *Decorative Cast Ironwork in Great Britain.* London: G. Bell & Sons, Ltd., 1960.

Little, Nina Fletcher. *Little by Little.* Boston, MA: Society for the Preservation of New England Antiquities, 1998.

Lindsay, J. Seymour. *Iron and Brass Implements of the English House.* London: Alec Tiranti, 1970.

The Manufactories and Manufacturers of Pennsylvania. Philadelphia, PA: Galexy Publishing Co., 1875.

Mary Ann Furnace. *Note Book,* 1850. Berks County, PA. Manuscript Group 2, Business Record Collection, Division of Archives and History, Pennsylvania Historical and Museum Commission, Harrisburg, PA.

Melling, Elizabeth. *Kentish Sources V Some Kentish Houses.* Maidstone, Kent, UK: Kent county Council, 1965.

Mercer, Henry C. *The Bible in Iron*, ed. Joseph E. Sandford, 3rd. ed. Doylestown, PA: the Bucks County Historical Society, 1961.

Miller, Harry. *Canada's Historic First Iron Castings*. Ottawa, Canada: Department of Energy, Mines and Resources, 1968.

Murdock, William Bartlett. *Blast Furnaces of Carver*. Poughkeepsie, NY: 1937.

Nessi, Luigi. *Antique Tools and Instruments*. Milan, Italy: 5 Continents Editions, 2004.

Nylander, Jane C. *Our Own Snug Fireside*. New York, NY: Alfred A. Knopf. 1993.

Parkman, Francis. *The Discovery of the great West*. Boston, MA: Little, Brown, and Company, 1869.

Patten, Matthew. *The Diary of Matthew Patten*. Concord, NH: Rumford Printing Co., 1903.

Pierce, Arthur D. *Iron In The Pines*. New Brunswick, NJ: Rutgers University Press, 1957.

Pine Grove Furnace. *Day Book*, 1825. Manuscript Group 175, Pine Grove Furnace Collection 1785–1914. Division of Archives and History, Pennsylvania Historical and Museum Commission.

Pine Grove Furnace. *Ware Book*, 1814. Manuscript Group 175, Pine Grove Furnace Collection 1785–1914. Division of Archives and History, Pennsylvania Historical and Museum Commission.

Pine Grove Furnace. *Waste Book*, 1785–1787. Cumberland County, PA. Private Collection.

The Plymouth County Directory and Historical Registry of the Old Colony. Middleboro, MA: Stillman B. Pratt & Co., 1867.

Ragsdale, John G. *Dutch Ovens Chronicled*. Fayetteville, AK: the University of Arkansas Press, 1991.

Raistrick, Arthur. *Dynasty of Iron Founders*. Newton Abbot, UK: David & Charles, 1970.

Réaumur, Rene Antoine Ferchault. *The Art of Converting Wrought Iron Into Steel & The Art of Making Cast Iron Malleable*. 1722. Translated by Anneliese Gr□nhaldt Sisco. Chicago, IL: The University of Chicago Press, 1956.

Robins, F. W. *The Smith*. London: Rider and Company, 1953.

Rome, Adam Ward. *Connecticut's Cannon: The Salisbury Furnace in the American Revolution*. Hartford, CT: The American Revolution Bicentennial Commission of Connecticut, 1977.

Sanders, Clyde A. and Dudley C. Gould. *History Cast in Metal*. N.p: Cast Metals Institute, American Foundrymen's Society, 1976.

Schaumann, Meri Lou Scribner. *Taverns of Cumberland County Pennsylvania 1750–1840*. Carlisle, PA: Cumberland County Historical Society, 1994.

Schubert, H. R. *History of The British Iron and Steel Industry*. London, UK: Routledge & Kegan Paul, 1957.

Singer, Charles, E. J. Holmyard and A. R. Hall, eds. *A History of Technology*, 5 vols. New York and London, Oxford University Press, 1954–1958.

Smith, David G. and Chuck Wafford. *The Book of Griswold & Wagner*. Atglen, PA: Schiffer Publishing Ltd., 1995.

Spears, James F. *A Picture Story of the House of Derr*. Lebanon, PA: Boyer Printing and Binding Co., 1973.

Swank, James M. *History of the Manufacture of Iron in all Ages*, 2nd ed. Philadelphia, PA: The American Iron and Steel Association, 1892.

Tritt, Richard L. and Randy Watts, eds. *At A Place Called The Boiling Springs*. Boiling Springs, PA: Boiling Springs Sesquicentennial Publications Committee, 1995.

Tyler, John D. "Cast-Iron Cooking Vessels". *The Magazine Antiques*, (August 1971).

Veit, Richard and Charles Bello. "Contact and Early Historic Period Archaeology in the Delaware Valley." *Journal of Middle Atlantic Archaeology* 15, (1999).

Wagner, Donald B. *Ferrous Metallurgy*, in Joseph Needham, Science and Civilization in China, v.5 part II, Cambridge: Cambridge University Press, 2008.

Wainwright, Nicholas B. *Philadelphia in the Romantic Age of Lithography*. Philadelphia, PA: The Historical Society of Pennsylvania, 1958.

Walker, Joseph E. *Hopewell Village*. Philadelphia, PA: University of Pennsylvania Press, 1967.

Walker, Lewis Burd, ed. *The Burd Papers*. Pottsville, PA: Standard Publications, 1899.

Weaver, William Woys. *America Eats*. New York, NY: Harper & Row, 1989.

INDEX